Within seconds, the assassin would be firing shots, and everything would go off all at once, bottles exploding, everybody screaming, and somebody dying...

HOME FROM THE SLAMS

It began the day Joey Gallo came home to President Street. After nine big ones in the slams, he was in no mood for bad news. He was coming back to his family, the *capos*, soldiers and around guys who made up the Gallo crew.

The first thing he wanted to know was: What had Joe Colombo done for his people while he was away? If the answer was "nothing," then what were Joey's people going to do for Joe Colombo?

To find out what actually happened—to find out how the Mafia really treats its friends and enemies —read this first truly authentic account written by an insider!

THE SIXTH FAMILY

THE
SIXTH
FAMILY

by Peter Diapoulos
and Steven Linakis

Foreword by Nicholas Gage

THE SIXTH FAMILY
*A Bantam Book / published by arrangement with
E. P. Dutton & Company, Inc.*

PRINTING HISTORY
*Dutton edition published April 1976
2nd printing May 1976*
*Literature Guide Club edition published September 1976
Bantam edition / January 1977*

ISBN 0-553-10295-8

Published simultaneously in the United States and Canada

PRINTED IN THE UNITED STATES OF AMERICA

To Joey and to my *own* family, especially my wife Kitty and my deceased father. These are the people I love, without whom this book would not have been possible

P.D.

To my wife Hildegard, *Der blaue Engel,* and my daughter Helena, an innocent bystander

S.L.

FOREWORD
By Nicholas Gage

I first learned the importance of Peter Diapoulos in the Gallo gang from Joey Gallo himself. It was in the spring of 1971 and Joey had just finished a nine-year stretch in prison when he called me at *The New York Times*. He was very friendly, complimenting me on my articles and books about organized crime. He said he wanted us to get together for dinner so he could talk to me about his thoughts on writing a book of his own.

I refused his invitation as politely as possible, explaining that I make it a policy not to socialize with organized crime figures who might one day become targets of my investigative reporting. I did not add that my reason for this policy is that Mafiosi are much more likely to turn violent against a friend whom they feel has betrayed them rather than a reporter who is only doing his job.

Joey wouldn't take no for an answer. "I know you're Greek," he said. "We'll hit the best Greek places in town. My best buddy, Pete the Greek, knows them all."

I told him I'd heard that a Peter Diapoulos was part of the Gallo gang but that he was a minor figure. "Someone's been pulling your chain," laughed Joey. "Pete's like another brother to Al and me."

I never did hit the Greek night spots with Joey; but in the next few months, while he became the catch of the season among certain segments of Manhattan's social and theatrical world, my sources in Brooklyn kept me posted on his comings and goings, and on most occasions Pete the Greek was at his side. On April 7, 1972, Joey's literary ambitions were blasted out of existence by a burst of gunfire at Umberto's Clam House in Manhattan's Little Italy. The only member of his gang with him was Peter Diapoulos, who was wounded but managed to return the hit squad's fire.

That gun battle was the beginning of Pete's ultimate disillusionment with the Mafia. "They shot Joey in front of his wife, his stepdaughter, his sister—violating every rule there is in that life," he told me later. "I began to realize that all the talk about honor and brotherhood that's supposed to be part of the Mafia is bullshit."

Nevertheless, Peter honored the code of silence and went to jail for a year on a gun charge rather than talk to authorities about that night at Umberto's. In prison his disillusionment grew when he learned that the Gallos were not taking care of his family as Mafia tradition required, nor were they doing much to avenge Joey's death.

Shortly after Pete was released from jail in the summer of 1973, I learned from my sources that he had reappeared briefly on President Street in Brooklyn at the Gallo gang's headquarters, and then vanished. In June 1975, I got a strange phone call at the *Times*.

The caller was a man who identified himself only as Greek-American and told me he thought he might be able to arrange an interview for me with Peter Diapoulos. I told him I'd be very eager to meet Mr. Diapoulos, and a few days later I received a call from the same voice which told me to fly to a certain city where I would be met at the airport. When I landed I was confronted by a Zorbaesque character with a Cretan mustache and curly hair shot with gray. He drove to a motel and advised me to request a corner room that didn't adjoin other rooms from which we could be overheard.

As my new friend and I were walking to my room, we were joined by a third man whom I recognized from his mugshots as Peter Diapoulos. He was short and muscular and walked with the elastic step of a fighter or a dancer. (Jeffie Gallo, Joe Gallo's first wife, later told me that Diapoulos was the best Greek dancer she had ever seen.)

While my friend tried to make small talk, Diapoulos said nothing. From my room I ordered lunch for me and drinks for my guests, and when the waiter arrived, Diapoulos hid behind the door, just like in the movies, while his friend checked out the waiter before undoing the door chain.

During that afternoon we talked about almost everything except the Mafia and Joe Gallo. As the two men left, Diapoulos said he would meet me for breakfast the next morning and tell me whether he would give me the interview. He made an appointment for 8:30 A.M., but at 7:30 my room phone rang and he told me he was downstairs. He had come early to check things out in case I had set up a reception committee for him.

At breakfast Diapoulos told me he would give me the interview, and he would get in touch with me to tell me when and where it would happen. During all my contacts with Diapoulos I never had any way to reach him but could only wait for him to contact me. When he decided to talk to a reporter, Diapoulos told me, he selected me because Joe Gallo had told him I was Greek and that I "played things straight."

During the next few weeks Diapoulos called me several times to set up appointments, which he later would postpone. Finally I was instructed to fly to yet another city and go to a hotel where I would request another corner room—a double. When Diapoulos joined me in the room he seemed a lot more relaxed and informative. He had made up his mind to talk, and we began taping sessions almost immediately.

This interview lasted for three days and two nights and during that time Diapoulos never left me. He slept in the room with me, selecting the bed farthest away from the window, and we ate every meal together in the hotel restaurant, where Diapoulos always chose an isolated table. Inside the room we spoke in English but outside we spoke Greek. Diapoulos' Greek, incidentally, is more polished than his Brooklyn underworld version of English, and I found him to be a good source. He was open and unpretentious. I learned that his children had no idea what his real name and occupation were and that when he took his son and daughter to see *Death Wish,* he was appalled by all the on-screen sex and violence. "I got them out of there fast," he said.

No investigative reporter would ever print a story without checking out every detail. I asked Pete a lot of questions and his answers all were confirmed by independent sources. When he didn't know something he said so, instead of making up an answer as informants often do. Most of all I was impressed by his honesty in describing life in the Mafia. The tales of treachery, pettiness, scrounging, bungling, fear, and exploitation rang true and were contrary to the more publicized notion of Mafia families as bastions of loyalty, efficiency, and underworld honor.

The honesty of Pete's story, as set down here by Steven Linakis, is tangible on every page. Pete was present at some of the most violent and most dramatic events in recent Mafia history and he remembers them with recriminations and anger, but nowhere does he exaggerate to make an effect or gloss over details he doesn't know. Peter Diapoulos may have done quite a few things in his life that he now can repent at leisure, but he doesn't lie. Maybe that's one of the reasons Joey Gallo liked him so much.

AUTHOR'S NOTE

The story of *The Sixth Family* is told in Pete "the Greek" Diapoulos' own voice. Some of the special argot may be familiar to readers of the many books about the Mafia published in recent years, but even Mafia buffs will find words and phrases that are either totally unfamiliar or have a different meaning than they might expect, as the argot is not only colorful but intended to deceive. I have therefore provided this short glossary of terms as they are actually meant, to help the reader as he enters the extraordinary secret world of the true Mafioso.

—*Steven Linakis*

AROUND GUYS—associated with the mob, but not in well enough to be members of a crew

BABBANIA—hard drugs

BIG TABLE—a meeting of the Mafia Council or Commission

BOOSTERS—thieves

CAGETTA—a guy who has the shakes; a trembler

CAPOS—captains

CLIPPED—killed or wounded

CONSIGLIERE—councilor or adviser; ranks between an underboss and capo

CREW—segment of a Family; sometimes it also means a Family

DOUBLE-BANG—double cross

FALL—arrest

FUGAZY—phony, counterfeit

GIRLFRIEND—pistol

GIVEUP—usually a trailer driver who pretends to have been hijacked

GOING TO THE MATTRESSES—holing up, armed with heavy weapons when a gang war breaks out

GOOD FELLOW—also commonly known as a "button-man," or the more familiar term: a man who has "made his bones," a man of respect. Also referred to as "the made guy," "made," or "the button"

GREENS—money

GUMMARE—mistress

HIGH BLEACHER—one who safely stays in the background and risks nothing

HIT PARADE—is your number to be hit (killed); the "hot" number is number one

KNOCKAROUND GUYS—not connected with the mob, but used by them. In most cases they are "boosters" with something to fence

MARK—generally someone conned, but it also means a "shylock" or a bookmaker not connected with the mob. As such they are "up for grabs" and can be taken by any crew, usually by extortion

MOD SQUAD—the younger element of the Gallo crew

MOVE IS ON—action against a rival or enemy is being taken

MUSTACHIO PETES or OLD GREASERS—the old timers of the thirties and forties, and earlier

OUTSIDE GUYS—although considered as part of the mob, they are only on the fringe; they do not have the status of "around guys"

RABBI—a spokesman who settles grievances and discusses Family business before the Mafia Council. Only a "good fellow" can appear before the Council as a "rabbi"

REGULAR—member of the first line of a crew, with the status of soldier with distinction; however a "regular" is not necessarily a "good fellow" or a "made man"

SHYLOCK—loanshark

SITDOWNS—appearances before a boss, usually involving a grievance; opposite sides must be represented by their "rabbi"

STREET PEOPLE—same as "knockaround guys"

TAKEN OFF—killed or wounded; sometimes also means being conned

TURKEY TIME—immediately before a shooting

UBAC (pronounced ooh-bac)—an old Sicilian con

UBATZ (pronounced ooh-batz, a bastardization of "upazzo")—meaning "crazy" or "the crazy one"

UNDERBOSS—ranks just below the boss of a Family and over a consigliere

VIG—the interest owed on a "shylock" loan

WASTED—killed

WHACKED—killed or wounded. "Whacked out" means killed, but "whacking out the greens" means dividing up the money

WORK or A PIECE OF WORK—sometimes a killing; sometimes a con or thievery

YAHM—a black man or woman

1971

one

Then in the winter Joey Gallo was coming home. Early that morning we waited in Armando's Café, not saying anything, nothing at all. Tony Bernardo sat across from me at the table, looking down at his shoes, as though he was asleep, while, Blast, Joey's kid brother Albert, was by the window, waiting for the backup car. He'd been there for some time, not saying anything either.

Armando the Dwarf* came out of the kitchen with that quick, short-legged walk. He was happier than I'd ever seen him. All he'd talked about since letting us in was Joey.

"Blast," he said, "when are you guys leaving to pick him up?"

Blast ignored him.

"Listen, you have to bring him by."

"Leave us alone," said Blast.

"You got to. We'll make it like an anniversary or something."

"Some anniversary," said Tony Bernardo. "What're you going to celebrate? The big nine and a

*Armando Illiano.

3

half he pulled in the slams?" Then he asked me, "Greek? Think Joey'll be like he used to?"

"It's too early to think."

"Yeah, too fucking early." He threw his head all the way back, smiling to himself. His eyes were still heavy from sleep, his hair wet and shiny like he'd just combed it. He was one of the regulars of our crew.

Finally the backup pulled up and parked. Out came Blast's nephew Stevie Gallo and Bobby Boriello, another kid from the Mod Squad. Louis the Syrian,* another of our regulars, a little guy in his fifties, was smiling. He was always smiling, today especially. He loved Joey. But the two kids weren't smiling at all.

Blast seemed worried. He had been running the crew. After today, we all knew who'd be running it.

He asked his nephew if he checked for law, then told him to go with Bobby B in the backup. We were going in the lead, going laundered, no pieces. The backup had the girlfriends—three thirty-eights and one thirty-two. Blast called that senior citizen protocol. He was some high bleacher, taking no chances.

When we drove off, Armando stood in the doorway, happily yelling, "Don't forget. Bring Joey around later."

It was the eleventh of March. Well, I wanted to remember that date, all right. If all those years in the slams hadn't taken the juice out of Joey, if he was only half the Joey Gallo we knew, it would be the start of some very heavy shit once he'd heard all there was to hear about Joe Colombo.

All the way to Hawthorne Circle, getting onto the Taconic Parkway with all the winding turns, we didn't say much of anything. Then Tony Bernardo started up again, wondering what Joey would be like after so many years. I said, "Maybe he's cooled for the better."

"Don't bet on it, Greek," said Blast. "Listen, all of you. I don't want anybody agitating Joey, filling his head with a lot of crap. So let me do the talking. I want him home, settled down for a week, before we give him the whole number."

*Louis Hubela.

"Some number," said Tony Bernardo.

"Yeah," said Louie the Syrian, smiling.

The road went winding and you'd see country. Crows were flying. There was something nice about it. But when we made the exit, going through the town, and then made that turn, there were the high walls of Sing Sing. Louie the Syrian was staring.

Before Blast headed for reception, to get Joey, he told us, "Remember what I said. Let me do the talking."

We waited a long time. Wind was blowing up stuff in circles. Then the door opened, and coming out with Blast was Joey Gallo, carrying a suitcase. He looked awfully small walking out that door. You had to see him. His eyes were deeper, almost skull-faced, the way I remembered his brother Larry. But then he was ten years older, the first time I'd seen him in all those years. He looked like a different Joey Gallo altogether, except for that mole on his cheek.

He just stood there, then hugged and kissed us, then squeezed my cheek, twisting hard. "Greek, you sweet sonofabitch," he said. That was the old Joey, giving me one of those crooked grins of his. Then his nephew hugged him, introducing him to the kid, Bobby Boriello. "What the fuck?" he said. Boriello, a big six footer, was wearing his usual wide bell bottoms and high heels, the coat with very wide lapels. His nephew's clothes were almost identical. "That's how they dress now? Like cunts?" And that, too, was the old Joey Gallo. I was as happy to see him as anybody. Still, I couldn't get over how bony his face had gotten.

In the lead car he looked back, then squeezed his eyes shut and shuddered. For a while he was a long way away. "All right," he said finally, and asked Blast to fill him in on the furniture business and the numbers action, but mainly on Joe Colombo. You could see that Blast was very reluctant to tell him Colombo had reneged on everything after the Profaci war, speaking only about everything but.

"But what about Colombo?" Joey insisted. "This car got no wire. We can talk."

"Joey," said Blast, "let's save it till we get home."

"Hey, Albert—that look. You're holding back."

"We'll discuss it . . . the proper time . . . when you're home and settled."

"I want to hear it right now, not later."

"All right."

"Now!"

Blast was like a cat around a hot plate of soup. "Well, there's Dolly."

"What about Dolly?"

"Maybe Nicky Bianco gave her the word."

"The word for what?"

Blast hated like hell to tell him. "To rip us off for thirty or forty thou."

Joey's eyes danced. *"What?* And she's still walking around?"

"That's about what Larry said."

"Hey, Albert, what the fuck has been going on? She had to get the nod from Colombo. You'd better start telling me everything, and I mean everything."

"Why can't you wait till we get home?"

"Right now! Start telling me!"

"All right. Before you get your piss hot—"

"I *am* hot."

"Larry and I never wanted you to flip over this and lose your good time."

"Come on!"

"Well, the promises after the Profaci thing."

"Give!"

"Colombo hasn't kept too many. No, that's not it either. He hasn't kept any, not one—nothing."

"Nothing?"

"Nothing but the buckwheat, the shit. Hate telling you when you're just coming home."

"Glad you are telling me. And I want you to tell me everything. Hold nothing back. And if we have to move on that fat cocksucker Mr. Joe Colombo, we'll move on him just like we did Profaci."

Blast looked at him as though for the first time, as though he came from a different century. "Joey, come on. What did that get us with Profaci? All it got us was Joe Colombo."

"Start telling me."

Blast told him some of the things that had hap-

pened since the old man, Carlo Gambino, had given
Colombo the Brooklyn throne, that we hadn't won any
decisions, only lost them. He dealt with the time their
older brother Larry ran the crew. Nothing had gone
right. Then after Larry died of cancer, nothing had
gone right with Blast. He told him about the time
Colombo had sent down word to lay off babbania (as
if we were heavy into it) and to lay off stocks and
bonds and hijacking, that it was bringing heavy federal heat. Then he told him, "Pete and I had to go for
the sitdown at his funeral parlor."

Joey looked at both of us. "You two guys went
to Colombo's? Where? The basement with the fucking
coffins?"

"We had no choice," said Blast. Then he told
him how we had to lay back, while all along the
Colombos were into stocks and bonds, heavy on babbania, because they wanted all the dough for themselves, and greens are power.

They talked about it all the way back to Brooklyn. Joey wanted to move on Colombo. Blast wasn't
very happy about that at all. He liked to reason things
out. Joey told him where reasoning had gotten him.
Nowhere.

At East Fourth Street the backup went around
the block. We followed, staying well back. Law was
on the block. The second time around we stopped at
the house. In the foyer Joey's relatives came at him,
wailing in tears, grabbing him. It was like an explosion. There were so many you couldn't get by. It
was just about everybody: Mama Gallo, aunts and
nephews, his pretty ex-wife, Jeffie, and his daughter.
Mama Gallo wailed the most.

"All right," he said. "I'm home. Let's cut out the
bullshit crying. Just show me what's there to eat."

I told his mother, "Put some weight on him,
Mama. He needs it. Give him lots of pasta."

"Listen," Joey said to his brother, "we got to talk
later. We still have a lot to talk about."

Afterward Joey was in a corner with Jeffie. She
was still crying, but laughing too. His kid was run-

ning around the place with some other kids. A lot more people came, friends and relatives, along with guys from our crew. It was jammed with people like an old Italian wedding.

Bulleye,* one of the around guys, had eyeglasses like the bottoms of Coca-Cola bottles, making his eyes enormous. I asked if he'd seen the rest of the guys. But I knew he was the wrong guy to ask. Everybody was over at Armando's, waiting turns to come over to the house. I caught my partner coming in with some people. Bobby Darrow† was very spiffy, and jittery as usual, smelling like he'd taken a bath in cologne. For a change he wasn't on uppers or downers. He wasn't even sauced.

Joey hadn't met him since I'd brought him into the crew. I introduced him when I got the chance.

"So," said Joey, "you're Bobby D. Hear the only one who can control you is the Greek. That right?"

"That's right."

"Hear you're good with this." Joey worked his forefinger, squeezing. "That right?"

"Right."

"Tell me, how are you related to Rocky M?" asked Joey, meaning Rocco Miraglia, a Colombo capo. Bobby told him they were second cousins, not too close or anything. Then Joey said, "But Rocky's over there, and you're over here. What do you think about that?"

Bobby shrugged. "He's there, I'm here. The only kind of work we ever did together was legit, for the *Times*."

"The New York Times?"

"Yeah. You know, route men on the trucks."

Joey grinned. "Stay close with my Greek."

The party lasted into the night. I wasn't drinking much of anything. I told Blast maybe it wasn't a good idea to stay too much longer. He wasn't drinking so much either.

Two guys stayed, while the rest of us went back to President Street, to Armando's. Armando was really excited, wanting to know how Joey was, how he

---

*Anthony Prano.
†Robert Bongiovi.

looked, everything. Even the law asked. Every hour two guys would go to the party and two would come back. Bobby Darrow and I went back and forth a couple of times. It was some night, a nice homecoming, except that we had to keep watching now.

two

Joey Gallo was in the slams when the Italian-American Civil Rights League picketed FBI headquarters in Manhattan, tying up traffic for blocks. While the FBI took pictures of wiseguys, Nicky Bianco, the Colombo capo, took pictures of the feds. When Joey heard about it, he told his brother, "Don't be a fucking jackass and picket. This is the most ridiculous thing that can happen. That Joe Colombo has to be an idiot to think he can get away with it." But Blast, to appease Colombo, had sent Mooney,* the only made guy in our crew other than Joey; Punchy,† a regular; and the Mod Squad. But the rest of the regulars and the around guys never picketed or signed petitions.

Well, Colombo called me down on it, wanting to know why I hadn't taken part, and there I was thinking, with feds taking pictures and making me, they would have come down a lot harder on my paper scores. You know, stocks and bonds. I had worked better than three and a half million in paper and once

*John Cutrone.
†Frank Illiano.

moved a million-dollar negotiable. The feds might
have had my prints on some paper but not enough to
stand up in court. If I'd gone there, screaming like a
jerk with a picket sign, they would really have come
down on me. So I told Colombo what was natural to
tell him, that I'd been on the lam with my partner,
that the feds would have nailed me and Darrow the
minute we showed up. He bought it.

Joey had heard about that, as well as the Feast of
San Gennaro, how the Colombos were getting Italians
to join the League and selling them hats. There were the
buttons too. One had "Numero Uno" on it and sold
for ten dollars. Another had the Italian flag, another
crossed Italian and American flags. These went for five
bills each. Then there were the coordinator buttons for
the first big rally at Columbus Circle. They went for
ten bucks. Joey said he now understood why Colombo
had been taking the blood out of our crew, the blood
from all the Numero Uno bullshit. With all the greens
going into his own kick, and all the publicity, Joey
was convinced Colombo was pushing for the big
throne, Carlo Gambino's.

Joey made his move the first week back. He told
Blast to set up the meet, but that the Colombos were
to come to them. We weren't about to get suckered and
go to the Colombos for the sitdown. The important
thing was getting all the promises straightened out, and
we weren't going to lose any decisions from here on
in. And from here on, he and Blast would never get
caught together. They'd walk in ones. If one got
clipped, the Family business would go on.

Then he heard all there was about Dolly from
Blast. That more than just bothered him.

About four years before he'd come home, his
brother Larry found out that two ledger books for the
numbers bank were missing. Dolly, who ran the bank,
wouldn't show him the two, saying they were around
but she didn't know where. Larry really flipped when
he found she'd ripped us off for at least thirty or forty
thousand. He told her she'd have to make it up, and if
it wasn't for her mama she wouldn't be walking. Mama

Rosie, before she died, had handled the bank. She was one hell of a lovely woman. When we had gone to the mattresses during the Profaci war, she cooked and took care of all of us. But Dolly did nothing.

She always had the hots for Nicky Bianco, the Colombo capo, and Joey was sure he had the forty-thousand-dollar prick. What really bothered him wasn't that she was probably reporting everything back to Nicky B. The real insult was that she had pulled a ripoff right in our own backyard. Joey said he had to chase the fat cunt off the block.

Dolly, all of five-five, and nearly as wide, had a foghorn for a voice and a bad mouth. Across from Roy-Roy's Café you could always hear her cursing longshoremen who gave her action, screaming at her daughters, or blowing off to her old man. If she wasn't blowing, she was beating the hell out of him.

Just as Joey was talking about her in front of Roy-Roy's, along came Dolly, blowing off like a horn to some longshoreman. Joey told the kid, Bobby Boriello, "Grab that fat bitch, take whatever she's got in her hand, bring it over here. Want to see what she's got there."

"Joey—"

"Do like I tell you to do. Just go over and take it off her."

Bobby took her arm and the strap of her bag. "Listen," he said, "what have you got there? Let me see."

"Whatta you mean see? Get the fuck out of here."

"The bag," Joey yelled. "Grab it from her." Bobby hesitated. "Do like I tell you."

Dolly wasn't giving up that bag. She pulled and he pulled. That big red fish mouth of hers was going off, cursing him silly. She tried to slap him and he gave her a push, yanking so hard that the strap broke. She kept on cursing and screaming until she saw Joey. Then she really got panicky. "Joey," she said, "what's going on over here?"

"Hey, cunt, get off the fucking block. Leave everything you got."

Dolly, her hands out, her hair roped and wild,

looking like some sloppy Medusa, said, "But, Joey, what're you talking—"

"Hey, I'm not going to repeat myself again. Move everything you got, *now!*"

Just then her old man stuck his head out the upstairs window. Tony Bernardo let go a couple of shots right by my ear. The powder stung, and along with the flashes I saw cement chipping over the window. Dolly's old man ducked back inside, the curtains flapping out. Dolly now had the cagetta, the trembler, screaming all over and not knowing which way to run. Finally she ran up her stoop. Her daughters were screaming in her apartment. Then they all ran out, Dolly's old man in front of them. Dolly had the metal box.

Joey yelled, "Get it!" and Tony Bernardo grabbed her, almost spinning her into the big café window. Her daughters were screaming, *"Animali! Animali!"* The old man wasn't yelling anything. He was just running.

The box had all the numbers and book action. We took everything we wanted from her apartment and turned Dolly's Café into our own club. Joey wanted the walls dark brown, the rugs gold, and everything else white. We were in Roy-Roy's talking about it when Dolly's son-in-law came in, a kid named Jerry. The kid made the mistake of mouthing Joey. Joey cocked him and threw kicks at him until I could get the kid away.

Joey's hand was cut bad by the kid's teeth. He was holding onto that hand. Somebody got him a towel and some ice. It left bloody marks. He needed stitches and a tetanus shot, but he couldn't make the hospital and chance a report. They'd have him back to Sing Sing for violating. I took him to a doctor I knew.

In just a couple of days Joey had gotten into a lot of things.

That week word came down that Colombo was sending his two capos, Rocco Miraglia and Nicky Bianco, for the meet. He couldn't have picked better people. Rocco looked like Colombo; and Nicky B, besides that business with Dolly, had been a Gallo during the Profaci war, and nobody liked him then.

Nicky Bianco, as a Gallo, had indicated to Joey's brother Larry that he could work a connection with Raymond Patriarca, the New England boss, about settling up the Profaci war and making peace. But if Nicky Bianco was to be our spokesman, our rabbi, he had to be a made—a good fellow.* Nicky was made, but not in the usual way, like after doing a piece of work, usually a killing. Blast (who never was made) especially resented it. We all did.

Everybody was down on him on President Street. We couldn't respect him, and he went to Colombo and asked to swing in with him. But he had to get the nod from Larry Gallo. Larry told him it was all right, but to remember he was a charter member down here, not with Colombo. And when he wanted him, he was to come. Nicky never had to. Now he was coming down as a Colombo with Rocco M.

At Roy-Roy's Café I waited by the door. Two of our people were across the way. I got the sign when the Buick turned the street. I called to Blast that they were here. You could see them in the big Buick, making the place. As soon as they parked and got out, they stood for a moment, opening their coats and jackets. They weren't carrying. You had to see that Rocco Miraglia. He had the stern look of Colombo's, the same build, everything, even the same slow swagger, the slow swing, except for that gimpy left arm.

Nicky B came in smiling. Rocco looked stern and somber as hell, eyeing out the place good. He didn't have that swagger now, and he was going cold. You could feel it. Nicky still had that grin, but he wasn't so damned comfortable either.

Blast shook hands with them, saying, "Hi, Rock. Hi, Nicky."

"Hi," said Nicky. "Hi, Greek."

"Yeah," I said. "Hi, Rocky."

Rocco M shook hands with me, looking past my shoulder. We led them to the back, under the archway.

---

*Once a Mafioso of good standing has appeared before the Mafia Council of dons, swearing always to be loyal, he is then made a "good fellow," and has won the respect of the entire Mafia community.

Joey was at the big round table, his arm in that white
sling. "Sorry I can't shake hands," he said. "But sit
down. Let's get this thing going."

Demitasse cups were on the table. Joey spiked his
coffee with anisette. Rocco stood eyeing Joey, then the
sling. Nicky pulled up a chair, saying, "Hey, Joey,
you're looking real good."

"And I'm feeling good, especially what I've been
hearing."

"Like you never been away."

"Hey, Nicky, save the bullshit. We're not here for
that shit. Rocky, sit down." After he asked if they
wanted anything, he came directly to it. "Nicky, the
reason I'm talking to you, and not Rocky here, is because you know exactly what promises Colombo made.
But none of it was ever fulfilled. Am I right?"

"Joey, you're putting me in a spot. I'm just here
to greet you, give you Joe's love and respect."

"Hey, Colombo wants to send his love down to
me? Nicky, get off that fucking shit. You know there's
no love between him and me. You know he never fulfilled the promises and obligations like he was supposed to."

"But I got an envelope for you. Joe just wants to
welcome you home, wish you luck."

"Sent me down an envelope? Yeah? Let me see the
envelope."

Nicky slid it across the table. Joey spun it around,
lifted the flap with his thumb, saw it was money, and
passed it over his shoulder to me. "Count it, Greek." I
counted ten one-hundred-dollar bills. "Nine and a half
years I did in the fucking slams, and he gives me a
thousand. Who the fuck needs this money?"

All the while Blast sat watching his brother. His
hand went out. "Excuse me. Nicky, Rocky, I want to
speak to my brother a minute. All right?"

"Yeah, sure," said Nicky. "Go 'head."

Over by the counter Blast told Joey, "What're you
doing? Whatsamatter with you? The nine and a half,
you didn't do it for Joe C. You did it because of your
own ignorance. You were told what would happen."

"Ignorance? Al, you just did an ignorant thing

pulling me away like that. Now they smell dissension between us."

"Joey, it's a good meet."

"Hey, Blast, I've been off the streets almost ten years. I'm supposed to be stupid about the way things are done now. But if you got off the high bleachers, got down there with the men, you'd know what was coming off here. Greek, am I right?"

"Joey, do me a favor," I said. "Keep it with your brother."

"Al, they're looking to sucker us."

"Well," said Blast, "at least let's find out what they got to say."

"Yeah, Al, Joe C's love and regards. Yeah, all right. Okay. Let's get down to the necessities."

Back at the round table he told Nicky B, "Listen, there's nobody who knows better than you what was said and what was supposed to be done in our peace movements with Profaci, the promises of Mr. Colombo, *Mister* Joe Colombo."

"Joey, excuse me. I'm in no position to discuss this now."

"There's nobody in a better position than you. You were our rabbi. That's got to be settled up and it's got to be settled up now. And I mean now. And Mister Joe Colombo is not sending for me or my brother. And he's not sending for any of my men when he gives the greaseball finger," saying it while he crooked his forefinger.* "Understood?"

"I don't under—"

"Nicky, I think you understand good. I don't have to make it any clearer. Colombo's not my boss. I'm my own boss. These are my men down here, not his. Relay that message to him. Relay that we want the promises settled now. You want to get back to me, you know how. Okay? There's nothing else I have to discuss with you. Just tell him like I told you."

Nicky's smile was gone. They stood up. Rocco,

*The worst moment in a Mafioso's life is when he is summoned to a meeting by the boss of his Family. This can result in a quickly executed death sentence for the "wayward" soldier.

as quietly as he could, said, "All right, Joey. We'll tell
him."

Joey threw the envelope over to them. "Take this
back to your boss. And tell *Mister* Joe Colombo I told
him to shove it."

When they started out, Joey said, "Wait a minute.
Leave the money. I'm broke."

After they'd gone, Blast turned to his brother.
"You can't do it any other way, can you?"

"Hey, Al, you're the politician. You can con the
Statue of Liberty to take a walk. But that Colombo's no
Statue of Liberty."

Blast shook his head. "You should have listened
to me. Now they'll move on us."

Nicky Bianco called Blast for a second meet. He
wanted to come down with Gerard,* another ex-Gallo.
Joey told his brother to go on the meet and to indicate
to them that we needed money, had debts, had to
straighten our Family out.

At the meet Blast was told that Joe Colombo was
in no position to discuss their differences now, as he
was too busy with the forthcoming second Italian Unity
Day rally at Columbus Circle and didn't want Joey
causing any problems whatsoever. Joey's answer was
that there wouldn't be any problems if the cocksucker
sent down a hundred thou. That was his favorite number. When that got back to the Colombos, we were
told that Joe C had nothing further to discuss with us.

Then Colombo went to the old man, Carlo Gambino, telling him Joey was going to be a big problem
now that he was out. But the old man told him it was
his Family, to take care of his own problems, correct
them, and not to involve others. This not only meant
the other four Families would stay out of it. It also
meant that Colombo could set us up for the hit parade, and nothing would ever be said.

We got the Twenty-One Club together up at Roy-
Roy's apartment. Twenty-one guys, all shooters. Joey
said he'd make us all good fellows, just like he'd been

*Gennaro Basciano.

made a button, and that he'd bring the outside guys
in, introduce them to everybody at the Council, Commission, or whatever the fuck the old greaseballs liked
to call it. Then we'd kiss and embrace them, as part of
us, our Family.

Well, we did all that. It wasn't legal, if it could be
called that. The whole thing was a goddamned farce,
only Joey was deadly serious. You never fucked with
him when he was serious. The thing he did say was
that from now on we were going to be Numero Sèi, the
Sixth Family, and from here on in none of his men
were being called for the fucking sitdown shit. We were
our own Family, answering to no one.

Then he said, "All right. Grease the pistols. The
move is on."

three

Now it was only a matter of time before we went to the mattresses, once the war started, and we needed bulk money to finance it. We weren't going to make the same mistake with Colombo that we did with Profaci when he had hundreds of millions and we had nothing by comparison and were outnumbered better than five to one. So we were out for heavy action: hijacks, marks, and kidnapping three big mob guys connected with Colombo. If we grabbed these three, we could bring in at least three hundred thousand in bulk capital.

They were essential to big numbers banks, heavy shylocking, and bookmaking. One big controller had between half a million and a million on the street. Take him out and the other two, and everything would stop. The Colombos had to have them back, and they'd pay.

The more we thought and talked it all out, the less we liked it. They'd connect it right off to us. This was one of the few times the Gallo brothers agreed on anything, and they decided to cool it. Instead we came up with the idea of putting the snatch on two bookmakers connected with us.

They were two brothers, two bookmakers from Fort Lee. A few years back, after Blast began running our crew, the two wanted to be disconnected. They felt we'd lost too many decisions for them, that they were paying too much for what they were getting, and they wanted to go in with somebody stronger, so they went to Mr. Gribbs,* the boss of the Harlem crew. Since the two wanted out, Gribbs told Blast that the only fair thing was to let them, provided they paid. Blast said if they felt like that, it would cost them fifty big ones and they'd be free forever.

The two brothers got the word back. They cried all kinds of poverty, but we knew they were taking heavy action, had a wire service, everything. For a week they yakked about it, saying how hard it was, excessive. But at the same time, they had made their intentions known and could find themselves disconnected from everybody and marks for any crew to take them off.

Then they said they had to go to a factor or a shylock for the greens. After they paid us, they weren't connected with Gribbs' crew or anybody.

We'd taken them off, that's all, and Colombo, since he was our boss, was in on it. A piece went to Mr. Gribbs, a bigger piece to Colombo. We cleared thirty thousand. It should have been a lot more. Colombo knew we needed it, and instead came off as usual like Profaci—all for himself. We got the double-bang and so did those two brothers because they were right back with us. There was no place else to go.

So we had no love for them anyway, and even if we had, thirty thou was thirty thou. Now we were going to make it another two hundred thousand, get a couple guys from left field to play the snatch, guys they never saw before. What was beautiful about it, we'd blame the Colombos. So would the feds if they were onto it. Everybody would, and after that the two brothers would need us all the more.

We talked about it over at Joey's apartment, and

*Carmine Tramunti, who inherited the Mafia Family of the late Gaetano Lucchese, known as Tommy "Three Fingers" Brown.

Joey laughed his head off, saying he could just see those two with the cagetta, squirming once they were nailed. Then Tony Bernardo said we should put the snatch on Colombo, like we once had done, and instead of five cents, get ten million. Joey stopped laughing and said, "Had that cocksucker good. Had him in my hands. Should have killed him then. Just knew I should have killed him."

He was talking about what had started the Profaci war, when we'd snatched Profaci's brother, Profaci's bodyguard, and the underboss. The fourth guy everybody—including the feds—had all wrong. It never had been Sally the Sheik.* It was Joe Colombo. And by snatching him that time, Joey, and he more than realized it, had spotlighted Colombo, and all because of Profaci.

Joe Profaci, who had all of Brooklyn, was the last of the old greasers. Besides all the mob action, he was one of the biggest importers of olive oil. Before he died I'd heard he was worth better than two hundred million, legit.

Profaci would give you the five-dollar wedding, the con, use you, then kill you. You could do a good piece of work, and he'd still kill you. Wiseguys feared him even more than Albert Anastasia, the Executioner.

I'd only seen Profaci once, didn't know that much about him personally, except that he had six kids and that when he got cancer he really got religion. He had a house in Miami Beach, but at Twelve Pines in New Jersey he had an estate covering more than three hundred acres that once belonged to some U.S. President. Profaci had his own personal chapel and even an airfield.

Two dons once controlled Brooklyn—Profaci and Albert Anastasia. Anastasia, who was getting too powerful, who had the nod from Lucky Luciano, had control of the Brooklyn and Manhattan waterfronts. But this went against Vito Genovese's ambitions. He wanted Manhattan all to himself, while Profaci wanted

*Salvatore Mussachio.

Brooklyn and the Staten Island docks. So Profaci and
Genovese decided to take off Anastasia, and they gave
that piece of work to our crew, designating Larry and
Joey Gallo and Joe Jelly.*

They did their surveillance, learning Anastasia's
routine from information passed on by Profaci and
Genovese. A week later Larry decided when and where:
a barbershop in mid-Manhattan. Before all that, they
approached Anastasia's bodyguard and read him the
rights. He had no choice with the big bosses in on it.
Either he walked or he'd be killed. The bodyguard said
he'd walk, and he did when Anastasia had the hot towel
on him. They took off Anastasia without any trouble at
all.

All three were made good fellows after that, except that when they went to the sitdown, there was one
thing bothering the council. Joey Gallo was called Joey
the Blond then, but he also had the name of Ubatz,
the crazy one. A good fellow could never be a user of
babbania, and a lot of people thought Joey was on
something. They weren't about to ask him to show his
arms. If he was being considered, they had to maintain
their respect. As tactfully as they could, they asked if
he would agree to stay in a room, with all the comforts
of food and drink, and not leave for two days and two
nights.

Joey stormed, but Larry asked him, "How can it
hurt? The tab will be on them."

So for two days a good fellow stayed with him,
watching. The Council was puzzled that he hadn't gone
into withdrawal, but was relieved too. So they made
Joey, and Joey always joked about that later, saying,
"Couple of days later all them fucking greaseballs re-
gretted it. They knew they'd made a big mistake."

Of all the Families, we were the outlaws. We were
called the international mob because there was a Greek,
two Syrians, an Egyptian, an Irishman, a Puerto
Rican, a Jew, and all the Italians. We never believed in
kissing a mob boss. We only kissed our own crew, the
guys we would die with.

*Joseph Gioielli.

Over the years bad feelings grew toward Profaci among the rank and file, not only our crew but all the others in his Family. Guys never knew if they were coming back when called. And while we were doing the work and getting crumbs, just the buck wheat, he was getting richer. No other boss treated his men this way, and finally we all moved on him.

At first everyone wanted it: Junior Persico's* crew, the Renaldi and Bat brothers, Vinny the Sidge, Abby, and a lot of other guys. With his entire Family moving on him, Profaci would have to come to terms.

But the first one to back out was the Snake, Junior Persico. Then Abby,† the Bat brothers, and all the rest followed when Profaci promised them a better share of everything if they stood with him against us and annihilated us all.

Well, we'd made the big move, all right, and there was no turning back when we grabbed the underboss, Joe Magliocco; Profaci's bodyguard, John Scimone; and Profaci's brother Frank. The fourth, Joe Colombo, wasn't worth the trouble and we were going to dump him. All we found out about him was that he was just into bookmaking and rigged dice games. He had less than six bucks on him and not even a decent watch.

Magliocco was a disgrace, whimpering as though we'd shoot him right there, and later whining that he was having a heart attack. Profaci's brother was so shook up, he shrank every time somebody came in the room. John Scimone was cool but shaky. He had good reason. He thought Joey crazy enough to kill him. And Joey was more than just thinking about it. He planned to. Colombo, though, was something else. He was the coolest of the lot, saying he feared dying like any other man, but if he had to go, he would go like a man. He asked that it be done quick and without torture, as that would be silly since he was nothing but a bookmaker with lousy action at that.

That really got Larry's and Blast's respect. It impressed Joey too. He often said afterward that Joe

*Carmine (the Snake) Persico, a capo.
†Anthony Abbatemarco.

Colombo had the biggest pair of balls of anybody. But all along he felt he had to kill him, kill all of them.

Profaci sent word down that he wouldn't negotiate until his men were released unharmed. Joey wanted a hundred thou before considering negotiations, and to show he meant business he said he'd kill one for a start and dump him at Profaci's door, that the only way to negotiate with Profaci was with a pistol to his head.

Larry was for releasing them, then negotiating. He thought we had won a round but that Profaci would win all the rest and kill every one of us if we killed even one of his people. They really argued, screaming at each other, and they damned near went at it. Rather than set it all off by Joey killing them, Larry sent Joey with his wife Jeffie to California.

For months Profaci made a lot of promises through Scimone and others, but nothing happened. John Scimone, mainly, and Larry had been into negotiations. Scimone said he had good news finally, that it was worthy of a celebration, and asked Larry to meet him at a cocktail lounge on Utica Avenue, right off the Flatbush extension. Joey hadn't known about it. He never would have let Larry go. Instead Blast argued with Larry, warning him that he was being suckered. Larry said he had to go, but if he was taken off, Blast would know what to do.

Just before opening that night, the cocktail lounge was dark and almost deserted, except for some guy running the bar. Scimone said the guy was all right, but this wasn't for his ears, and took Larry to a booth. In the next one, laying under the seats, were Junior Persico and Sally D,* while out in the alley with the car, working backup, was Apples McIntosh,† a mean mick-Italian, who was Junior's right hand.

Larry had just set down his drink when the rope came looping his neck. He came back over the partition, kicking, seeing those big owl eyes of Junior's. Kicking, he caught Scimone in the face. The life was

*Salvatore D'Ambrosio.
†Hugh McIntosh.

going out of him, then he let go, pissing and crapping himself.

Just then the law came in on them. The sergeant saw Larry's feet. Junior and Sally D ran past, pulling pistols. Outside there were shots, the cop in the sector car getting shot in the face. Scimone lay in the gutter, a cut over his eye, his cheek bruised. He didn't know how he got there. The bartender didn't know any of the guys, didn't know what was coming off, didn't even remember bringing over drinks or what anybody looked like.

Then Joey Jelly had disappeared. It turned out that Sally D had met him leaving his house. The old greaseball message came back to Jelly's wife, wrapped in his shirt, the fish: He sleeps with the fishes.

We went to the mattresses, keeping a lot of shotguns and rifles around. The law never made that I was affiliated then. Larry wanted it that way. They could hardly move. The law and the feds were on them with roll call, accounting for everybody, and when somebody wasn't around, they wanted to know where and why. I could move, all right. Boarded in at my apartment, I kept hand pieces and a lot of hardware.

By the end of that year, we were low on greens. Joey had this mark, Teddy Moss, who was into shylocking on the side, but without the connection. Joey went on him. But Moss had gone to the DA, was wired, and Joey was nailed for extortion, hit with the big seven and a half to fourteen.

In the slams the Profacis had tried to nail Joey. They put ground glass in his chow, sent big guys to work him. Joey almost bit off one guy's tit, and another time bit off a guy's ear. Then he got himself in with the blacks and Puerto Ricans. Nobody came in on him after that.

The following year Profaci died of cancer. Magliocco took over the Family. He had not forgotten the humiliation, when he whined for his life, and he was going to make us all pay for that. The war kept on. Guys were taken off on both sides, and we were getting the worst of it. Then there were the runaways, who you never saw again, and the turncoats, who first went over to the Profacis, then over to Magliocco.

All that time, Larry Gallo wanted Junior Persico, who had tried to kill him, and the rest of them really bad. He was obsessed with it. For months he had to wear a scarf to hide the rope burns, and every time he'd look at those burns he'd tell you how badly he wanted them all dead.

He got this demolition expert, this kid, to rig Junior's car, to set it off by remote control, and picked himself, me, Punchy Illiano, Nicky Bianco, and Gerard to be his backup.

Well, over on New Utrecht Avenue, Junior wasn't about to walk out from his bar to his Caddy. He took a good, long look around, then checked his car to see if he could spot anything. If he had just raised the hood, the kid would have thrown the switch, and it would have gone off in his face. Instead Junior got in, and before he even turned the ignition, the kid threw it.

The car went right off the ground, doors swinging open, glass breaking everywhere, metal clanging down. You could feel the explosion right inside your chest. Nobody could have lived through it. We got the hell out of there.

But Junior, the sonofabitch, wasn't dead. The explosion had gone down, not up, and Junior had only gotten a concussion. We found out later that he'd checked into a hospital using a phony name. Junior was stunned, staggering we'd heard, and for days he thought his hearing was gone.

A couple of months later we tried again. We laid for him at his gummare's, one of us up on a roof with a walkie-talkie, and two others in the panel truck. When the guy with the talkie saw him coming out, he called. The panel truck blocked Junior's car at the curb. The back door swung open, and a shooter fired for his head and chest, catching him with three slugs, one through the mouth, coming out his neck, and two in his arm and hand. Junior was hit bad. The sonofabitch still lived. He was the Snake, all right. Still, his arm was paralyzed.

Then Magliocco died of a heart attack, and Joe Colombo, out of nowhere, was moving for the throne. He was the only one who actually profited from that long war.

I guess before he died Profaci noticed Colombo when we'd kidnapped him, and John Scimone probably had some good things to say about him. So when Magliocco took over the Family, I imagine Colombo was in good enough to find out that Magliocco had sided with Joe Bonnano in his move to dominate the Commission by taking off the two most powerful bosses, Three-Fingers Brown* and Carlo Gambino, who had succeeded Albert Anastasia. Colombo was not only cool, he was smart. He knew that Gambino, sooner or later, would be Capo di Tutti Capi, Boss of Bosses. Colombo, betraying Magliocco, went to the old man and told him what was coming off.

As vicious as Profaci was, old man Gambino was just the opposite: a quiet man, but nobody to fool with. One thing, he repaid loyalty and never forgot a favor done, or a vendetta. So when Magliocco died, Brooklyn was up for grabs, and the old man, now the big boss of all, gave Joe Colombo the Brooklyn throne.

Larry and Blast felt very comfortable about that. They respected Colombo. Colombo, it seemed, respected them and said that the Gallo grievance was more than justified. Gambino was very pleased with that and got everyone to the table for the sitdown.

Raymond Patriarca, the New England boss, was brought into the negotiations as mediator, and Nicky Bianco was our rabbi for the sitdown. Colombo promised a new regime, a fairer slice, a fairer shake on everything. It was a solemn obligation and was to be the end of the Profaci way. But Colombo proved to be no different from Profaci with respect to keeping it all for himself.

And now that Joey was home and we were moving

*Gaetano (Tommy "Three-Fingers" Brown) Lucchese.

on Colombo, it was as though we were moving on
Profaci all over again, as though the war never ended.
This time, though, we'd have the greens to keep it
going. This time the first to get whacked out would be
Joe Colombo.

four

At Dolly's Café one afternoon Joey Gallo sat in the back, well away from the windows. This old lady was being escorted over to him, her face so wrinkled it was like a spider web. She was shawled and all in black. I didn't like seeing all that black. The young guy who held her by the arm had a hairlip and a mustache that tried to cover it. He spoke first to Joey. He was very nervous. He wouldn't look at anybody.

It turned out that somebody was ripping off mailboxes, and they had gotten two of the old lady's social security checks. The young guy said the police would be useless and wanted to know if Joey could do anything. Joey told them that was federal, and they should go to postal. The guy said they would be useless too.

We were over at a table when Tony Bernardo and Punchy Illiano came over. Punchy was another of the regulars. He was in his early forties, sort of good-looking but tough, with a lot of graying hair. "Whatsamatter, Greek?" he asked me.

"Nothing. What should be the matter?"

"Heard you guys made a big paper score," said Tony Bernardo.

"How is it," said Bobby Darrow, "that it always gets around so fast?"

I kept watching the old lady. I don't know why. You don't see much of her kind anymore. In the old days you did, but that was all over. Now it was mostly Puerto Ricans. Red Hook had gone seedier and was even more crowded than before. The only Italians left, it seemed, were the ones too poor and too old. She was the last of her kind. Sometimes I felt we were the last.

The old lady had gone a little hysterical. Joey pointed a finger to her face. "Aspet. I said I'd take care of it. I know you're angry, and you have reason to be, but I'll take care of it. Rely on me, have confidence, and just leave your problems in my hands. I'll find who is responsible, and he'll repay you, with interest. I will see to it. Here," he said, and reached into his pocket, coming out with a fifty. She was very proud and wouldn't take it. He said, "You have to eat," and passed it to the young guy. He was reluctant about taking it. She still wanted to give it back. "Hey, I'm going to get angry, Grandma." Joey touched her face. "It's only a loan. When I get your money back, and I will, you pay the fifty you owe, that's all."

Then she accepted it. She started to kiss his hand but he took it away. He didn't go for the old Mustachio Pete crap. Just call him Don Giuseppe and you'd find out. Instead he kissed her hand. "Now go home, Grandma, and don't worry."

A car pulled up front. I could make out Blast and his gummare, Bitsey, but I couldn't make out who was in the back. Then I saw that it was Sammy the Syrian* and Cousin Tony.† Tony was a disabled ex-fireman who'd been caught with his ex-cop brother shaking down some whore. His brother had been bounced off the force, while Cousin Tony got a big slap on the hand. He was an around guy. Sammy the Syrian, a regular, was the tall guy with the big stomach.

*Sam Zahralban.
†Anthony DiBernardo.

Blast and Bitsey seemed to be arguing. She was probably after him for money again. She was always digging into him for that. She was flash, blonde, shapely, and mean. Nobody liked her very much. She never came around to Dolly's when she knew Joey was there. She was taking a chance. Joey would abuse her.

Blast stuck his head back in the car and passed her some money. She smiled.

"Hey, Greek," Joey called. "You sweet sonofabitch. Come here."

He really gave that smile of his when I laid the attaché case on the table. It was a fair paper score, better than twenty grand. Blast as always was there first, coming out with the usual about how he had his expenses.

"Hey, Al," said Joey. "Get off that shit. Don't be like some fucking tightwad."

Blast was getting more and more like that, all for himself, or else it was that Bitsey who was driving him. I think that was when Joey and Blast started going bad on each other.

"Come on, Greek," said Joey, rubbing his hands together. "Whack up the money. I mean, you are giving me a piece, aren't you?"

"How much you figure?"

"Who's greedy? Any generous contribution will be greatly appreciated."

I checked the door, then started whacking out the money in bundles of hundreds and fifties. Blast wanted more for expenses.

"Al, Al," Joey said. "It's the Greek's work, his idea. He's the boss. Right, Greek? Now you sweet sonofabitch, give me mine."

I saw the way Blast looked at me. Well, things were a lot different now that Joey was home. Just then Tony Bernardo came by hissing, *"Feds!"*

The money, attaché case, everything was gone by the time the two feds came in. The little one with the topcoat and glasses I knew as McCoy. The other I didn't know. He looked like a football player just after a haircut.

McCoy looked around at the dark brown walls, the chairs white and modern. "Who fixed up the place, some beatnik?"

Joey gave them the usual "What brings you around?" and McCoy said, "Nothing much." They even shook hands. You'd have thought they were the best of friends.

It had been only a couple of weeks since we'd made the move on Colombo, and the feds were already onto it. They were coming around a lot heavier than usual, city law too. Joey would rap with them for a while, and it would all be very friendly.

When they laid on the block, Joey would send somebody out to invite them in, saying that even though they were law, they were human beings and it was shit-ass cold out there, and maybe they'd enjoy a nice cup of coffee and, anyway, they could hear better inside. I never saw one of them get sore about it. In fact, it got so it was like open house. All sorts of law would stop by, sometimes taking their coffee with a little anisette. Joey's attitude was they had a job to do, and we had a job to do.

One night we were sitting around at Dolly's, playing gin rummy and watching the time, when the feds came in again, McCoy and another new guy. Bobby Darrow didn't even look at them as he waited for me to pick a card. "Here's roll call," he said.

McCoy smiled. "How are you, Pete?"

"All right," I said. "Anything I can help you with?"

"There's a lot you can help us with. Where's Joey?"

I shrugged.

"And Blast? I know—you don't know."

"I don't."

"Heard Joey's going to remarry Jeffie."

"Yeah," I said, waiting for Bobby to draw a card. "Come on. Pull the fucking card."

"Heard she's a regular cuckoo clock," said McCoy.

"Who?"

"Jeffie."

"She's all right." They were behind me, looking down at my hand, just standing around in their top-coats, but taking in everything. "Can I get you anything?"

"Anything, something I can give Mr. Hoover."

"Coffee maybe?"

"Fine."

"What's he want, your partner?"

"Wants more than coffee," said McCoy.

I called over to the kid taking care of the tables. "Two coffees for these gentlemen." Everybody in the place kept looking away, saying nothing, but throwing down the cards hard. The other fed was very uncomfortable. "You'll get used to it," I told him. Then to McCoy, "He's new?"

"Sort of."

The new fed wouldn't take his coffee, but McCoy spoke into his when he said, "Heard you fellas have made the big move."

Bobby, looking down at his hand, said, "Do we look like we're moving? We're right here."

"Where's Cutrone and Hubela?"

That was Mooney and Louie the Syrian. "Around," I said.

"Their turn?"

I said nothing.

"On surveillance?"

Bobby flicked the cards off his chin a couple of times. "Greek, he thinks we're law."

"When they're around," said McCoy, "you guys aren't. Or it's Punchy Illiano and Tony Bernardo. Pairing off?"

Bobby said to me, "Don't understand this guy."

"Me neither."

Then McCoy said, "Heard Joe Colombo was down a couple of weeks ago."

"Down where?" I asked.

"Roy-Roy's Café, when Joey slapped him."

"Slapped who?"

"Come on, Pete."

"Have you seen Colombo down here lately? So how could Joey slap him?"

"Heard it that way."

"Joey cocks," said Bobby. "He don't slap. You got a fucked-up wire."

"All right already," I said. "Play the hand."

"I am," said Bobby. "Playing it just like them."

McCoy seemed to be enjoying himself. "So Joey's made the big move. Pleases a lot of people."

"Like who?" I asked.

His smile went wider, then he put down his coffee cup. "Well, thanks for the usual. Tell Joey and Blast we were around."

It began to rain. Outside, by the windows, people were hunched over and running. You could feel the rain when the two went out the door.

As they left, Bobby finally looked at them. He snapped his thumbnail off his teeth. It meant a number of things, none of them any good. "Cute mother-fuckers," he said. Then he was by the door.

"Still see them?" I asked.

"Yeah. Sonofabitch, it had to rain."

It was coming down harder. The feds were still laying on the block, parked in a car by Armando's. Their wipers were going. There was nothing to do but wait. I called my wife in the meantime. She knew about the phone being tapped. All she talked about was the kids. She said she'd wait for me to call her later. When I got off the phone, the feds were still there.

In the parking lot, Darrow and I waited in the Caddy, in the rain. The rain kept coming down like a bastard. Then we saw the headlights of the panel truck turning in.

Bobby Boriello was driving the panel. He parked and called in the back. "It's the Greek and Bobby D."

" 'Bout time," I heard Little Ang Parfumi say as he opened the side door of the truck. What hit you was the closeness of the thick fiberglass and mattresses. Inside you could just make it and them out. Louie the

Syrian worked his hands through his hair, while little
Ang rubbed his forehead and ears as though it was
prickly from the fiberglass. He was short and bony,
one of our regulars. If he could weasel you, beat you
for money, he would. Joey had nicknamed him the
Worm.

Little Ang said, "Took your sweet-ass time re-
lieving us."

I told him about the feds laying on the block, that
we had to make it out the back way, so we couldn't
come right down, not unless he wanted the feds to help
us.

McCoy had it right. We'd been pairing off, making
surveillance. We had discussed using both the garage
and showroom roofs of Kaplan's Buick on Eighty-
sixth Street. The garage roof, set back, was ideal for
catching Colombo outside the luncheonette off the
corner, and you could make your escape by the side
street. The showroom roof midway was better for covering the whole street, and you could clip him either at
the luncheonette or at the real estate office, almost
directly across the street. Still, you'd have to make it
from the roof, then around all the new cars on the lot,
before making the side street. Colombo had to know it
was a good place to lay for him. He wasn't about to
move that way.

We'd first thought of using a car, drilling out the
trunk lock, putting in an eyepiece. A guy would move
the car, park it, and lift the car's emblem covering the
eyepiece, looking right down Eighty-sixth or at his
house, his gummare's house, or in front of his funeral
parlor. A shooter could lay in the trunk, but it wasn't
any good if someone came up from the sides or from
the front of the car. Then, if they made that eyepiece,
the emblem sticking up, they would have loaded up
and shot up the car.

The panel truck was better. We lined the walls
and roof with thick fiberglass and put mattresses on the
floor to muffle the shots. Then we put one-way windows in the rear and sides. You could look out, but
nobody could look in. Behind the driver, solid ply-
wood, with a peephole to make the front. We would

work it the same as the car, the driver pulling up, parking, then taking a walk for a couple of blocks where a car would pick him up. We'd use the walkie-talkies to keep tabs on what was going down, and there'd be two shooters, instead of one suffocating in the trunk of a car.

Joey and Blast had liked my idea, so we had set up the panel truck over at their furniture store and tried taking shots from it. With the fiberglass and mattresses, you could hear the shots, but they sounded more like thumps inside a padded steel drum. You didn't get that heavy recoil, not even with a double-barreled shotgun.

That night, after we relieved Little Ang and the Syrian, we drove the truck to Colombo's funeral home. It was still raining. What I didn't like was that the funeral parlor took up the whole block, and across from it was nothing but an empty lot. If we were made, we'd have to run across the wide open lot or chance it with a truck that any car could outrun.

They were having a wake. With all the cars, you couldn't see anyone too well under the black, shiny umbrellas. They wouldn't be Colombo's people anyway. Cars came and went. It never was Colombo. There was no sense laying there, no sense at all. Then I thought I saw two Colombos getting out of an Olds, and I forgot about thinking there was no goddamned escape or anything else. One was the Snake, Junior Persico. It was him, all right, the big owl eyes, that wide forehead and skinny face. The other was Apples McIntosh.

Junior shook hands with some of the people on the porch. Then, after they had gone inside, I saw this kid coming along, leaning into a couple of cars, trying the door handles. But he had only tried two before getting to us. Then I saw Apples out on the porch.

I passed the scoped Remington to Bobby Darrow. The kid was by the cab, trying the handle. When he went on, he didn't try any others. Then he was on the corner, like he had to think about it, and came back, trying the handles on the side and back, coming around to the other side. Then he was trying to see in, cupping

his eyes with his hands. He went to the back and tried
to look in there. Then he went off, whistling. Apples
stepped on a butt and went inside. I buzzed twice on
the talkie and had Bobby Boriello pick us up.

After that we never tried the funeral parlor. Maybe Apples had sent the kid. Maybe he thought we were
the law laying on the block. Maybe the kid was just
into lifting the truck. Maybe nothing. That funeral
parlor was no damned good.

So we tried Colombo's house. His street was lined
with two-family houses mostly. Colombo's was a split
level. There were three cars outside: two in the driveway, one behind the other, and another by the curb-
ing. He had to be in there. Nothing much happened
until we saw this white Mark IV come on the block.
There were at least four guys, and they were looking.
About ten minutes later I saw the same car, coming a
lot slower this time. Its brights went on. They'd loaded
up. Chills went all through me. Bobby threw the bolt on
the rifle when they suddenly started barreling toward
us. They were going to let go. You could feel it.

I pulled Bobby down to the floor. But they went
right past. They were at the far corner, their tail lights
going bright red as they made a squealing turn. Everything was pounding inside me. Coming along now was
a sector car, its tires hissing in the rain. The two cops
didn't look or slow down by the truck. Then another
prowl car turned up by Colombo's house just as five
guys started out. Right behind them two guys flanked
Colombo, one holding an umbrella over him.

Bobby snapped his thumbnail off his teeth, then
leveled the Remington. "We cowboy?"

"Wait."

One of the guys had gone over to the sector car
and was talking to the cops, while the others got into
the first car. Colombo and the other two got in the
second. It looked like Colombo, with that swagger, the
slow armswing—only the left arm was held half-
cocked, held up almost to his side because it was
gimped. That wasn't Colombo at all, but Rocco Miraglia. Bobby knew it too.

I buzzed twice on the walkie-talkie. "Get us the fuck out of here, *now!"*

So there it was. Colombo—who had at least five shooters with him all the time, never following a pattern, so that the only place you could lay for him at all was Kaplan's Buick—now had Rocco M for the stand-in shot.

We began to talk about other ways to nail Colombo. There had to be a way. Then we discussed clipping him at the second rally he'd planned at Columbus Circle. He'd be standing still. He'd be set.

Maybe we could get into an apartment in one of those high rises or a roof facing the circle. Only there'd be feds and an army of cops, even a helicopter. They would figure a long-range shooter. We'd be made before we could move, and there wouldn't be any escape. From the high risers, the feds would be taking pictures with lenses a yard long that would show up the pimples on your nose, or they'd be right in with the rally, coming off like reporters, ice cream vendors, or even wiseguys. A roof or an apartment wouldn't be any good. The rally wasn't any good. It just wasn't feasible. Still, there had to be a way.

five

One Tuesday I went over to Armando's Café when Armando the Dwarf came by, pulling at my pants leg. He had his chest out a little, like always, and he'd tilt his head when he looked up at you. He asked if I'd seen Joey, saying that since Joey remarried Jeffie and moved to Fourteenth Street in Manhattan, he wasn't seeing Joey as much as he'd like. I told him he was enjoying married life, that's all.

Punchy and Tony Bernardo were kidding him, when this chintzy blonde—six feet tall with her platform shoes—came over to their table. Tony B told her Armando was our bodyguard, while Punchy told Armando to give her a little kiss. "Only with her standing, where you going to kiss her?"

Just then Blast went by the front window with some guy who owned a cocktail lounge, and eating place off Borough Hall. He was short, his jacket couldn't close over his big belly, and he had a wide stride, or it was just the way he swung his arms.

Once inside, Blast jerked his chin at me. At the table he said, "Greek, you remember Arturo."

"Sure," I said. "How are you?"

We shook hands. "Not too good," he said. He spoke with an accent.

"He's got a problem," said Blast. "Let him tell you. Listen, I want to see you after."

After he'd gone, Arturo said, "Have not see you for such a long time."

"Well, you know how it is. What's wrong?"

"Much. You know this—*come si chiama*—Fat Matt?"

"Fat Matt from the Harlem crew?"

"Hey, you think I ask? He break my face. Say he make much trouble for me."

"Slow down, Arturo. Tell me what happened."

"I try to tell. I am too excite."

What I got out of him was that this Fat Matt went on him, telling him that Arturo's waitress, the one Arturo had been making it with for the past month, was married to some wiseguy, and he had to know that you don't mess with a wiseguy's wife, *gummare,* or anybody, especially the wife. But when he said Fat Matt was going to Arturo's wife, who was so crazy jealous that she would kill them, I told him, "Aspet, walyo. Arturo, he's just shaking you down. That's what it sounds like. Who's the waitress?"

"Rosa."

"The one with black hair, really black and long, and the nice curves to her?" He nodded fast. "Who's she married to?"

His hand circled. "Hey, I no ask."

"Rosa fucks for everybody. Don't you know that? How can you get involved with a pig like that? Does this Fat Matt know you're a friend, an old friend?"

"Hey, he break my face I say something."

"You've got to tell him. Once he's told, that's the end of the trouble. Didn't Blast tell you that?"

"Sure, but—"

"Listen, you've got to tell him or he'll come down hard on you. He'll really weigh on you. I know him. When are you seeing him again?"

"He only say pretty soon."

"Do like I tell you, or he can be one mean mother."

"Eh?"

"He can be very, very bad, like some mustachio Pete, like Profaci. Worse."

"Hey, you think I not know this? I am much afraid to say something."

"You'll have to. Tell you what. When he comes around again, and he starts with the shit, here's what you do. Give us a call at Dolly's, and rest assured he'll never bother you ever again."

"Okay, I say. I tell him."

Blast came over. Arturo wanted to buy us and all our friends a drink, then invited Blast and me to come down to his place with our wives and the children for a good dinner and good wine. He took Blast's hand as though he would kiss it. Blast shook hands with him.

After he had gone, Blast said, "Well?"

"Won't be any trouble," I said. "When Fat Matt comes around again, Arturo's going to call."

"Good. Come over here. There's something I have to tell you."

We moved to another table, well away from everyone. I knew what was bothering him, and he said it. He didn't want me spending too much time with his brother. He wanted Joey staying close to home, not coming up with impossible things and then bouncing all over town. I asked if he was going to tell his brother that. "Blast," I said, "I'm not telling Joey I can't. He doesn't take 'can't.' You'll have to tell him. You know already what he'll say. And when he calls me, Blast, I'm going."

After Joey came home, there wasn't a day practically that he didn't call me, asking me to bring along Bobby Darrow. Well, I'd known Joey since we were kids—when Brooklyn, believe it or not, was a pretty place, when it had had nice green things and trees and nice houses—and we'd rap about the old days like they were coming back, whether it was about the time he got into a fight in the schoolyard and I went in to help him because he was such a little bastard, or about palling around with Mike the Bandit. Well, we'd rap about things like that, and he'd ask, "Whatever happened to Mike the Bandit?" and I'd say, "Don't know. Maybe he went straight," and Joey would say, "Maybe he was sensible."

Or he liked to kid me, not only because I was twice in the army, once as a minor, but the second time around I was in Austria as an M.P. You know, a military policeman. Well, I couldn't help that. I couldn't help where they stuck me. They just stuck me there. He thought it was the funniest thing he'd ever heard, a wiseguy an M.P. Once he asked me why didn't I get in with the Effen-Bee-Eyes. "We'd have some wire," he said.

Sometimes we talked about Teddy Moss, the guy who pinned the extortion rap on him, how a guy like that had to be taken off. But that was one thing Joey was reluctant about even considering, since the conditions of his parole were that if Teddy Moss so much as got a slap in the mouth, Joey was back inside for violating. "That's only if I'm not taken off," Joey once said. "But if I ever am, Greek, then you take him."

But what we really talked about was now, how to get Colombo up for the hit parade. That was heavy stuff. At the same time he was bouncing all over town as though he was making up for lost time. Well, he had a lot to make up. I really loved the guy, and I wasn't about to turn off on him. Joey would have to tell me first.

When Joey heard Blast was trying to pull me away, as well as other guys, control the men his way, Joey didn't like that at all.

Blast may have been a high bleacher, but he was a tough bastard when he wanted to be, and cold headed about it too, not going off like a pistol. I did have a lot of respect for him, as close as a brother while Joey had been away, and even before that. But there were some things about him that I didn't like. The guys felt the same way.

Not only was he tight with the greens, and Joey had tagged him with Tightwad, but he had a lousy

way of talking down to you. He'd say, "I can't reach
you. I have to get down to your level, if I'm ever going to be able to communicate with you at all." You'd
feel humiliated even if you were a complete moron.
That may have been shit, but it would bother you. But
there were other things about him.

About three months before Joey came home, he'd
brought in this John from the old Bonnano Family,
who knew all the protocol and Blast had him acting as
our consigliere. What didn't sit so good with everybody, we had to make appointments to talk to Blast,
and this John did something within the immediate
Family which I don't even like to mention, but was
reason enough to take the sonofabitch off.

Then when we moved on Colombo, and this John
knew a lot of shit would be going down, he came
around President with a bullet hole in his car, saying
somebody took a potshot at him. It was enough to get
hysterical laughing, because we all knew what Blast
would tell him, to go home and stay low. John, that
sonofabitch didn't want to be around when we'd really
have potshots taken at us. Some consigliere he was.

Then serious things happened when Blast turned
us away from whacking out three guys, guys you had
to clip.

One was Jackie Clark, a Gallo who defected.
Another was Larry Pistone, a Gambino, who'd dis-
graced us when he took up with Stevie Gallo's wife
after they'd separated. But one in particular was a
numbers runner named Tony. During the Profaci war,
he'd eyeballed Ali Baba,* and Ali Baba was tagged
coming off a pier in Jersey. Joey had to avenge his
death.

Ali Baba the Egyptian, was one bad dude, who
could crack your head open with one hand with no
trouble at all. Back then, he was Joey's man when he
wasn't working the ships as a merchant seaman. They
loved each other, and he was Joey's best man when
Joey and Jeffie were first married.

Well, Joey had set it for me, Sammy the Syrian,

*Ali Hassen Waffa.

and Roy-Roy* to go on this Tony. He often came into
Sammy the Syrian's bar, then tried the card and dice
games Sammy had going in his club next door. Sammy
was to invite him over to the club, and Roy-Roy and I
were going to take him off there. Everything was set
until Blast got Sammy and Roy-Roy to back off. That
really set Joey off against Blast.

Then Mooney started sending feelers out to get
the guys away from Blast. Mooney, the made guy, had
been Larry's partner. He may have been a little bald-
headed guy, as small as Louie the Syrian, but he was a
tough oldtimer, and he was making his move, trying to
get Bobby Darrow and me to come in with him. He
told me afterward that Blast had been flipping that I
was sticking with Joey. I couldn't help that. "Well,"
Mooney said, "if you're ever nailed, he's not going to
take care of you or your family. That's right, Greek.
You've got to think about that."

"Joey's not saying that," I said. "He'd never let it
happen."

"Yeah," said Mooney, "so long as Joey's alive."

Well, with all that, I almost forgot about Arturo.
One day he called at Dolly's, and he said he was
"much excite." I told him, "Hold it," that I'd call him
right back. Ten minutes later I called from a public
phone.

It seemed that after he told Fat Matt about us, Fat
Matt came down on him hard, smacking him across the
mouth, saying he didn't give a good shit about the
Gallos and he wanted his five grand by tonight or
Arturo was going to wake up one morning and find
his restaurant all burned down to nothing.

"Tell you what you do, Arturo," I told him. "Call
and tell him to meet you at Dolly's tonight."

He didn't like that at all.

"You want him in your place?" I asked. "With a
lot of people? What we have to tell him has to be pri-
vate. And rest assured, there's not going to be any
trouble. Understood?"

*Rosario Musico, a regular.

He still didn't like that, not any of it, and didn't want to call. I told him we'd call, and I'd be back to him when it was arranged, assuring him that there wouldn't be any trouble at all.

That night I got everybody out of Dolly's except Blast and Bobby Darrow. Arturo came in first, looking around as though he expected Fat Matt to jump out at him. He held a handkerchief across his cheek. I took his hand away. He had some welt across his face. "The sonofabitch," I said.

Bobby Darrow checked to see if law was laying on the block, then turned down the lights, except for those by the coffee urn and liquor bottles on the narrow table along the wall. He had his jacket off and his sleeves rolled up, but he had put a thirty-eight under the towel by the coffee urn.

Arturo was very worried that we'd do something. "Hey," said Blast, "zito-zito. Nothing's going to happen. The Greek told you. We're taking care of the problem."

Arturo wanted a drink. We gave him one, then another, and he kept watching the door.

Then Fat Matt came in, just big and dark. Bobby locked the door right behind him. Stopping at a table by the coffee urn and bottles, he tipped his hat to us. You had to see him. It was fairly warm out, but he had his topcoat draped over his shoulders, his gloves in his hand, the big pinky ring, the big cigar, and his fedora turned up on one side, like he was Al Capone. Blast stood behind us at our table. "You believe this guy?" he said.

Fat Matt took the table by the urn, shrugging his topcoat off his shoulders as he sat down and laying it on the chair alongside, his gloves on top. He clicked his fingers to Bobby, ordering a drink.

"The balls of this guy," said Blast. "Give him the fucking finger." Then to Fat Matt, "Hey, gumba, you're wanted here, not there."

Arturo touched my arm.

I said, "Blast, I told Arturo there wouldn't be any problems."

"From that clown?" said Blast. "There won't be."
Then to Fat Matt, "Let's go, gumba."

Fat Matt seemed to snort, took up his glass, his
pinky out, drinking slowly. With that same swagger,
he came over and sat at our table. Arturo tried to look
away.

"Tell us what you're drinking, Matt," I said, "and
we can get down to business."

"I have my drink. I am now for the business."

"You know what, gumba," Blast said to him.
"You even talk like an old greaseball. And I don't particularly care if the Greek said that you're here to talk
things out, discuss things in a nice way."

Fat Matt looked over at Arturo, taking him all in,
then eyed Blast and me. "Discuss what?" he said.
"What have I got to discuss with you two? My business
is with him."

"Hold it, Matt," I said. "You're here to discuss
things nice, or you're going to find yourself with one
big problem."

"What big problem?"

"You're uptown people. Am I right? You don't
even belong here, and you're coming down on a friend
of ours. Your boss never sent you on him. He doesn't
even know about it. Now if you want that big problem,
numero uno, with the table, going for the sitdown and
all that shit, and since you're all wrong, you can find
yourself up for the hit parade."

"Oh, yeah?"

"Come on, Matt. You know that. You can't be
that crazy."

"He's got no respect for my friend. He has to be
taught. He tell you about Rosa, that he's been fucking
her, when she's married to my good friend?"

"What good friend?" asked Blast.

"Teacher. You know him."

"Listen," I said, "we didn't even know Teach was
married to Rosa. Sure we know Rosa, but we didn't
know that, and I know Arturo here didn't know. He's
not that crazy to make it with one of ours. I can tell
you he is a man with respect."

"You can tell me, but he's still going to pay."

"Matt, you're just shaking him down. That's not right, and you know why it's not. You've got to be reasonable. We want to be reasonable, but you're not about to pull a shakedown on him. You got no respect for us when you're here just to talk and you're packing. That's an insult, when we're trying very hard to be reasonable. But you're fucking packing."

I cocked the piece under the table, laid it on top, my hand over it. "Now, I'm just going to ask this once. We do this reasonable, or with fucking pistols?"

Arturo went sick. His face looked like a dirty white sheet. Fat Matt didn't do anything except sit back in his chair. He was even smiling. He said it, and he said it quietly, "Greek, you're going to have to use that fucking thing."

"What?"

"You heard me, you Greek cocksucker." All the while he was reaching.

Blast came down on him, grabbing his hand. I came over the table and pushed Blast off him, jamming the pistol into his chest. He went back five feet like he'd been scalded when I let go, firing twice.

The biggest surprised look was on his face, his hand tearing at his chest, his fingers filling with blood. His hand came away and he fell over on a table, taking it and chairs over with him to the floor, his legs and arms going every which way.

Arturo let out a scream. Blast grabbed him, smothering his mouth with his hand. He wanted to run, but Blast had him, pushing him down in the chair. Bobby pulled Fat Matt all the way to the back room by the legs, the blood smearing a trail. I turned off all the lights and checked the door. Bobby took my pistol with a towel, wiping it down. Arturo was going into hysterics.

I said, "Listen, Arturo. Listen. We're getting rid of the piece. We're getting rid of the guy. Nobody'll ever know he was here. Nobody."

Blast didn't have to hold him now. His handkerchief was squeezed to his mouth. I took his shoulder. He was shaking so much, his shoulder was jumping. "I know, Arturo. I know. Not good to see a man killed.

But it's all over. Understand? We know what to do. Nobody'll ever know this happened, except us."

I could feel him staring at me. You just knew he had the flutters bad. "Listen," I said, "Bobby's going to take you right home. He'll stay with you till you settle down. But nothing to no one."

"Not even your priest," said Blast.

"The problem is over, solved," I said. "Understood? Say you understand."

His handkerchief came away from his mouth. He couldn't say it. He couldn't say anything.

Blast was by the door, waiting to open it. Bobby Darrow had Arturo by the arm, holding his hat under his chin in case he threw up, taking him outside to Arturo's car. When they'd gone, I poured a drink for myself, one for Blast, and a stiff one for Fat Matt, who really was Crazy Ang, a Greek from Greek Town.

Arturo, the mark, fell right. All that cost him twenty big ones. First he got up five thou, then ten, then another five. The "body" and the car had to be taken to a crusher in Jersey, where they would be whacked down to a square no more than a foot and a half across, then melted down so nobody would find bone or dentures even. After all, Arturo didn't want to be implicated in a murder. All that was very expensive to arrange.

We tried it after that with another mark, a guy named Genco, playing it the same way, and even doing it much better. I don't know what went wrong. But there was Crazy Ang, as a guy named Bimbo Tubs this time, sticking the pin attached to his pinky ring into the condom under his shirt just over his heart, the chicken blood flooding him, and giving a squeeze, squirting, after Blast "shot him" for a change.

We went to Genco's place, a nice bar and grill, and told him what we did to the body. He didn't say anything and went along wiping down the bar, then setting up drinks for us, saying this was not the time to talk about it, that he was very upset over what had happened, that he'd call that night. He never did. When we came by again, his place was closed. He wasn't anywhere. Sandy, a girl we'd used to work him, said he might've gone running to Miami.

The sonofabitch wrote us a letter finally. He said he hoped everything was going well with us and all our friends. He respected us and asked that we'd respect him as he knew, and praised our entertainment. He didn't explain how he knew except an old Sicilian would know an ubac, an old con.

The money for the ubac, like other marks and everything else, went into the war chest. But what I never realized then was how an ubac might have figured into the Colombo shooting.

six

Toward the beginning of June, about two weeks before the banchetto, the second rally at Columbus Circle, we were all over in the Red Hook section of Brooklyn pulling down the league's posters telling everyone to stay open that day and not attend, that it would be an insult to us, an insult to themselves.

Most of the time you got no static, and if you did you just asked if they had good fire insurance or told them how rough some of these local kids were. We'd say it was a lousy thing to mention, but a businessman had to be realistic.

Usually store owners felt they were caught in the middle, that if they didn't attend, Colombo's people would come down on them, and if they did, we would. The answer was very simple. We were a lot closer to them than the Colombos.

Then we called practically every pizza parlor in Brooklyn, Queens, and the Bronx, saying only that we were friends, that we weren't going along with the Colombo program, and advising them not to, that it could lead to serious consequences, problems they didn't need. Then we'd ask about the hospital, and all the rest that Colombo promised, all the money they'd put up for it. Where did they think it was? There never would be a hospital, or anything else. Colombo was making damned fools of all the Italians who were genuinely involved in the league. It had started off right and would have been good, but now there was nothing good about the league at all.

If Colombo, once he really got it working, had backed off and got somebody with a respected name up front, it would have worked for everybody. The league had been very persuasive. Politicians became jittery about losing Italian votes, and they squeezed the Justice Department to issue orders that terms like "Mafia," "Mafiosi," and "Cosa Nostra" were never to be used. Even the law had to worry about your civil rights and wouldn't pat you down so often to see if you were packing. We didn't have to do so many tricks stashing the girlfriends.

Colombo among others tried to get the TV show *The Untouchables* to knock off using so many Italian names. Then he worked on the people making the movie *The Godfather* not to use "Mafia" or anything else like it.

But that wasn't all. Some guy working on *The Godfather* made a speech on television explaining how the movie represented a small segment of Italian life, and how hard-working and industrious most Italians were, how they contributed so much to America, mentioning many fine Italians and those who were famous. But behind him you saw the guys with the big pinky rings. Any idiot would know they were mob guys.

Old man Gambino, who in the beginning had gone along with Colombo—when he did see the political pressures it could bring on the feds—started to get rattled with all the TV appearances Colombo was making and asked if he'd become an actor all of a sudden.

Maybe Colombo thought he was bigger than the old man, even bigger than the government, when he flipped that time his kid got collared by the feds for melting down silver coins. Colombo, screaming, started the business of picketing FBI headquarters in Manhattan. That was his big mistake. Must have been the best thing that ever happened for the FBI. They were taking pictures of guys that they'd probably never made before. But J. Edgar Hoover had his people coming down hard on every one of them.

They could only walk in ones and twos, and there was no way you could do any real business with the feds on you. All the Families were affected. Gambino and others, even some of Colombo's own Family, tried to get Colombo to back off, but he wouldn't listen to anyone. That in itself was setting himself up for the big hit parade.

In the first rally a lot of people attended from every Family, but the second banchetto was something else. Stores stayed opened, and the other Families boycotted. The teamsters and waterfront people stayed away as well when Gambino sent out the word. Less than half as many people turned out for the second rally. But before noon that day Colombo got shot in the head by that black guy, Jerome Johnson.

I was home when a special bulletin came on in the middle of a TV show. My wife, Kitty, almost in a panic, called me down from the bedroom to watch it. I just caught the tail end, seeing people scrambling, people in those green, white, and red hats, chasing some black guy, the cops holding several back, trying to push back others, cop brass atop the green riot wagons, waving and yelling. Then the camera jerked over a white, stocky guy on the ground, laid out on a stretcher. I saw that big, balding head and the blood going down his neck, and I knew who that was, all right, before the announcer said it. Then something about a black assailant.

"Black?" I said. I was half asleep as I watched it, and I said to my wife, "A black guy shot him?"

"I don't know," said Kitty.

The crowd was chasing a black guy, the camera going jerky, seeing sky, then barriers and feet, and I wondered if that was the guy, but they said that the black had been shot dead. Then a closer look at Colombo, and somebody trying to wave the camera-man away. I told my wife, "I'd better tell Blast."

He lived down the end of the hall. He was in his bathrobe, yawning. "What're you waking me up for?"

"Turn on the TV. Turn it on. Colombo just got clipped."

That yawn stopped, and his face changed alto-gether. "Where?"

"The rally? You kidding?"

"Turn on the TV."

"Oh, Christ. Your place laundered?"

"It will be, don't worry."

"I'd better call Iovine. They'll be pulling us in. Does Joey know?"

"Don't know. Just got it on the TV."

"Call, see if he's home. Tell him to stay in the house till we get there. And you'd better start calling the guys in. Tell them to head over to Armando's. Better start calling right now."

I got back to my flat and told my wife, "Kitty, call the super. You got a suitcase for him. You'll be right down. No questions. Give him a twenty."

I really moved, packing the walkie-talkie, binoculars, and a couple of pistols with boxes of shells, and throwing some clothes over that to keep it from rattling.

My wife was shaky. "Pete, what's going to happen now?"

"Did you call the super?"

"Yes. What's going to happen?"

"I don't know," I said, closing the straps, passing the suitcase over to her before making my call to Joey.

Joey and Blast were both picked up for questioning, and their attorney uncle, Joe Iovine, went to the station house to get them afterward. We offered, but the law said they'd have more than adequate protection, that they'd bring them back to President Street.

The crew was all waiting at Armando's when Joey came in, throwing his peaked cap as far as he could, saying, "What a bum rap they're laying on us over here. We clipped Colombo. Wish to fuck we did. But

that J. Edgar must be creaming his fucking pants. He's
going to have his own banchetto tonight."

We still didn't know if Colombo was dead or
what, but we knew that everyone would lay the shooting on us, and that we would have to tighten up. We
were all up for the shot now.

We didn't even get into who this black guy, Johnson, was or who might have sent him in, except to say
that the way it was done the guy had to be crazy or on
babbania. It was that crazy.

They really laid the shooting on us. The law was
saying that Gambino had paid Joey forty thou to take
off Colombo, and the big thing was that Joey had
been so tight with the blacks in the slams, that blacks
had come around to President Street before and after
he'd come home and, supposedly, they were there to
soldier, and that he might have psyched up this Johnson
to do the piece of work.

What horseshit. I would have known if we'd sent
Johnson in for the shot, even if Joey was working it
on his own, because there wasn't a fucking thing we
didn't talk about. Sure, he'd gotten close to the biggest blacks in the slams to keep the Profacis off him.
And he was always sending word down to his brother
and Papa Gallo, telling them that this or that black
dude was good people, had done him favors, and now
he wanted to reciprocate.

Blast said he'd try to get them jobs, but he never
really tried. The only exception was a black named
Slim who was very tight with Joey. As much as he dis-
liked doing it, Blast set Slim up with a thou for numbers action and put him on the honor system, checking
his ribbons once a week, without Slim having to come
around to President Street. He explained that he didn't
want to mess him up with the law since he'd just made
parole. I think, more than anything, he just didn't want
him around.

Joey still kept sending the blacks around. It finally
got to Blast. Joey told him to unhinge some of the
greens he'd been hoarding, or talk to some of his big

political friends, like that big asshole Mayor Lindsay, to get them jobs.

Even when Joey came home, and the blacks were still coming around, not one got in with us, with the exception of Slim, and he wasn't anything heavy or a soldier to begin with. Joey just liked people with real balls, and he didn't care what color they were as long as they were standup people. Sure, he laid bread on the blacks who came around and tried to get them legitimate work, better than the peon jobs they had to make parole.

He had one reservation about the blacks, though. He'd seen them come on like maniacs in Auburn during a riot, and he understood why, living in such a hypocritical country as this. But give some of those bad mothers pistols, he'd say, and they'd be looking to shoot some white dude who never did anything to them —shoot a guy for something somebody did to them twenty years ago, or something some rednecks or the KKK did to their uncle or old man. You couldn't blame them, he'd say, and he had real feelings for them, but he was concerned that they'd go around shooting up the whole town instead of tending to business. It was bad enough he was supposed to be crazy, than have some blacks soldiering who were crazier than him.

Well, that was the main reason a black never got in with us, even though we had practically everything else. And if by some chance Joey had thought of using somebody like Johnson to clip Colombo, the last thing he'd do would be to allow blacks to keep coming around President Street. Still, it was all pointing to Joey and our crew. It had to be a setup using Johnson. It was too obvious.

Despite the law coming out with the bullshit that Gambino had paid Joey forty thou to take off Colombo, they couldn't tie Joey to Johnson or any one of us. Gambino hadn't even discussed it with us, or given us the nod. We knew one thing, Gambino—or any of the other Families—wouldn't have been very unhappy if we had, as long as it was done the right way. And we wouldn't have risked having them coming down on us for the way it was done, shooting a guy in front of his family and friends. Since we'd considered every possible way, including the rally, we knew sooner or later Colombo would be so involved, that he'd do something stupid. That's when we were going to take him off.

There wasn't one black from Joey's time in the slams who tied in with Johnson. There was no tie-in with any of our crew, either direct or indirect. It was the Colombos who tied Johnson to us, and you had to figure they would. So I wasn't at all surprised when I later read in the newspapers that Joe Yak,* the Colombo consigliere, figured I'd set up the shot.

The way it got back to me was that I'd been seen with this colored broad and this Jerome Johnson just a couple of days before the shooting, and this same broad was with Johnson at Columbus Circle. The Colombos even had a picture of her and Johnson minutes before the shooting. They probably got it from some press photographer.

Well, if I was working the guy, would I see her and Johnson in the open, where a lot of wiseguys would make me with them? And what was she doing at the circle if this was the comeoff? Watching Johnson clip Colombo?

Still, that was the way Joe Yak tagged me, so I was number two on their hit parade. Joey was the hot number one, and Blast number three. Well, I wasn't about to sit down with Joe Yak and explain it. Let him think anything he wanted. Our main concern was that all the Families would come down on us if they believed, or if old man Gambino did, that we had anything to do with it. If they believed it—and that's what we really worried about—we'd all be dead inside of a week.

We had to do our own investigations, working out who had the most to gain, and who this Jerome Johnson was in the first place. We worked out all sorts of theories.

One was that it could have been the Colombos themselves, throwing the blame on us. Another theory, a good one, was that it was ordered by Carlo Gambino.

*Joseph Yacovelli.

The old man had good reasons, not only because the
league was screwing up Family business but because
Colombo eventually, with all the power he was getting,
would move on him.

The old man could have set it up in a lot of ways.
One was working a con. Johnson had done time, was
into pushing babbania, but was no user. Maybe the old
man worked an ubac with a phony federal narc, and
the comeoff of a bust. Some guy, naturally, would
take off the narc, and there would be Johnson implicated in a murder. But instead of taking him for bread,
they'd get him for the big favor.

Another theory was that Johnson might have
wanted some heavy action, or he wanted in with some
crew. Well, he could have gotten the five-dollar wedding, the con, been wined and dined, then told the action he'd be getting if he did a favor, a very important
favor, and if the comeoff fell right, he'd become a very
respected man.

Then working out the plan, the press pass, and
the professional camera, to pose Johnson as a newspaper cameraman, promising him big backup and escape.
It would have taken very big backup, somebody very
big to convince him. That was another way.

A fourth theory was that it was Abby. And that
was a possibility since Abby had the vendetta for our
crew for having taken off his old man, Frankie Shots,*
fifteen years before, so we could get his numbers action. Well, Abby, a Colombo, still had Bedford-Stuyvesant with twenty banks or so, ten very big, while we
had seven, and only two considered big. But Abby
had a lot of blacks handling his action. He didn't want
just the Colombos coming down on us. He wanted all
the Families down on us after the disgrace of how
Colombo was hit.

It might very well have been Abby, setting up
Johnson with an ubac, or playing him with the five-
dollar wedding, then double-banging him with the
second shooter to keep his mouth shut.

The other thing that some were saying was that

*Frank Abbatemarco.

Johnson was a loner, a psycho. But he wasn't into the
Muslims, Black Panthers, or anything like that. And
even if he was, what was there to gain? Start a Mafia
war with the blacks? Then he was a knockaround guy,
and knockaround guys give less than a fuck about politics. But to make the whole thing come off like some
political assassination? Something just wasn't right.

We'd rap about it a lot, and one time over at
Joey's new flat Blast came up with the Abby theory,
that Abby had set it up to look like we did it to get
even with us for killing his old man. "Let's think about
this," he said. "What kind of treachery did we pull,
taking off his old man? It's quite possible Abby's done
one better. Wasn't Frankie Shots supposed to come in
with us before the Profaci war broke? The backer with
all the greens? Only he was too smart. He stayed out of
it. But Abby was trying to get his old man with us,
and it would have been a different thing if we had had
the greens and everybody stayed with us. So what did
we do? We took off Abby's old man and threw it on
Profaci. And didn't Abby go crazy, wanting to get
Profaci no matter what? But then he found out that it
wasn't Profaci. It was us.

"But what did Abby do? Nothing. Maybe he was
just waiting for his right time. With all his action, he's
making two million plus a year. Maybe three. He's kicking into Colombo, and he hates Colombo for glomming
into him, but he hates us more. And he's got to figure
a way, and he's been sitting on it for years, figuring
out the best way, how to take Colombo off and throw
it on us. So who's he got working for him? Blacks.

"Now he knows, just like everybody else does,
that Joey was tight with blacks, and a black taking off
Colombo would automatically be thrown on us. And
he's got the bread, he's got the power to work somebody like Johnson. This is credible. And now, just like
we sat back when we thought it was Profaci who clipped
his old man, he's sitting back, waiting for everybody to
come on us, not just the Colombos—and that's exactly
what he wanted. Anyway, it's a neat theory. Joey,
don't you agree?"

"Who the fuck knows?" said Joey.

We went over the whole thing again, about Abby, the old man, and everything else, and about Johnson, the knock-around guy who's been in the slams, who'd had some action with babbania, who wouldn't sucker so easy with an ubac, who'd smell a double-bang coming off. Even with the old man, or Abby, he'd smell something and run. Punchy said maybe it was somebody so big that he couldn't run, like he'd been kept in the slams.

Then Punchy came up with the ubac theory again. "Only," he said, "let's turn it around. Let's just forget Abby and the old man a minute.

"Now here's this yahm, this bad dude Johnson, really into moving babbania. Maybe he got the good connection, some badass he met someplace, and the badass is onto real prime, and Johnson knows how to move it. Are you ready for this? Johnson's so greedy, he's not thinking straight, and maybe this dude coming up with the prime is federal, but no narc. He's Hoover's man."

"That's ridiculous," said Blast.

"What the fuck is so ridiculous about it?"

"Now it's Hoover," said Bobby Darrow.

"Maybe the CIA, all right?" said Punchy.

"Listen to this guy," I said. "He's in the middle of the Atlantic Ocean."

"Drowning," said Blast.

"Listen a fucking minute, will you?" said Punchy. "Johnson's a pusher. So what's more natural for him than to take on good stuff. How often does it happen that some fucking little underling gets onto prime? So he sees a chance to make some real bread. He doesn't have to deal with mob guys. He's got it direct, and he can move it before anybody lands on him. Only the law lands on him. They come in busting down the door. Now the big dude, he's got the big pistol. He lets go, a fed is down, shot dead, and that's heavy, none heavier. And they've come in from everywhere, from the fucking windows yet, and there's pistols all over them, and they're not fucking moving now. You see the picture?"

"Yeah, yeah," said Bobby Darrow.

"So what's wrong with that?" asked Punchy.

"Plenty," I said.

"Well, it's just a theory now," said Punchy. "We've kicked around a lot of stuff—Abby, the old man, everything. Now let me interject some other fucking thing. Them CIA guys."

"Now he's really going all over," I said.

"Yeah? Them CIA guys, don't they put the arm on people, snatch them, sometimes clip them, and don't they have the second shooter to clip the first so he don't blab?

"That piece of work on Colombo, that was a mob hit? Think about it. Put your marbles together and *think*. This stunard, this fucking Johnson, he's got the press pass, the professional camera, and he shoots. Where'd you ever hear of mob guys doing some dumb shit like that with all the law around? Tell me. Where? In the fucking movies? But the CIA, that's how they do it. And who are they asshole buddies with? Hoover. And who does Hoover hate the most? Colombo. So are you fucking thinking?"

Punchy, just because we all called him that, wasn't back on his heels. He'd been a middleweight and a good one, and sometimes he made a lot of sense. But this was crazy.

Joey had the biggest grin you ever saw.

"Joey," Punchy said, "ain't that possible?"

"Sure, like everything else."

"Who can buy that shit?" asked Tony Bernardo.

Mooney asked, "But what the fuck has the CIA got to do with Hoover? Who the fuck would believe that?"

"That's just it," said Punchy. "That's what is so beautiful about it. Nobody. But Hoover, *Hoover* especially, had everything to gain having Colombo clipped. Am I right, Joey?"

Joey was by the window. He didn't say anything. I told him to get away from the window. No telling who was across the way.

"Now let's get on this fucking Hoover," said Punchy. "Now, here's a guy that's really going bananas with Colombo's people picketing the FBI. And how do we know this? The way he sent the feds down on everybody who picketed. Here's this stunard, scungil, Colombo, going on the biggest man in Washington next to the President, and in some ways he's bigger because he can do no wrong. But Colombo, now, he's eating Hoover's balls. So what does a guy do when he's got the power? He starts figuring. Not good enough that nobody can move. He wants blood. He comes on like a Profaci, a beautiful double-bang."

"Hey," said Roy-Roy, grinning, "now J. Edgar is like Profaci."

"What's the difference?" asked Punchy. "One's legal, the other's illegal, that's all. But just say he arranged the Johnson ubac. All right, just say he did. Then have Johnson clip Colombo in front of his family and his fucking friends. Result. A big mob war. Colombos are on us, and we're on them. Main thing is Colombo has been taken off. Now listen to what I'm telling you. That's exactly what he wanted. Not only is he going to sit back and watch us killing each other, but there won't be any more stunard league. With Colombo taken off, is there a league? It's finito. Call me crazy, call me anything you want, but that's what I *really* think."

It gave us something to think about, that it was crazy, and we argued back and forth. Punchy wasn't only in the Atlantic Ocean. He was in the Pacific and Indian, bringing in the wildest, craziest things I'd ever heard. Christ, Hoover was into clipping Colombo. Maybe with a little help from the CIA, not to mention the President, Army, Navy, and Marines.

Yeah, I'd heard things about J. Edgar. A lot of people did. There was always some ex-fed who wrote a book, telling you what a miserable bastard he was, crazy in the bargain, crazy with power. But to have his people set up Johnson to clip Colombo—the CIA, as Punchy told it—was just too much for anybody to buy.

Joey hadn't said anything while we rapped it out. He'd grin most of the time, and wave his hand as if we'd all gone nuts. Afterward he gave me one of his grins and said, "Wild, isn't it, Greek?"

"Wild isn't the word. Next he'll be bringing in NASA."

"Makes us all pretty desperate, grabbing at anything, doesn't it?"

"Why not? We can't do anything about it anyway," I said.

seven

The day after Colombo was clipped, we tightened up. Within a week's time we extended the front of Dolly's by about six feet past the building line, giving us two doors, one small window on each side, and two small round convex mirrors out front so we could check both ends of the street from inside. Then we put wire mesh inside all the windows and doors to keep out grenades.

We were into buying heavy weapons: machine guns, rifles, shotguns, hand grenades and silencers. We tried to get the best silencers, the ones the army issued to rangers. A round going off would no more sound than if you clapped your hands, not like an ordinary silencer which made a pistol sound like small firecrackers going off. The armory, where we had the connection, stocked all the latest weapons, but not those special silencers. So we had a machinist make a couple for pistols, tried to make one for a rifle, only it wasn't perfected. You'd really hear every other round.

Joey and Blast were never to be caught together, especially now. Whenever either of them went anywhere, they were with at least two other cars. We also kept rotating cars and never took the same route twice in a row. We switched bridges all the time and rarely used the tunnel, where you could get suckered. Or, if we laid up, Joey and Blast had to know where we were. Once a day you had to call in or come down to Dolly's. And we were never to travel in less than twos and threes.

Jerome Johnson had more than just spoiled our plans. Joey told us at Dolly's, "All right, it's done. Now it's happening. But I'm telling you now. If any of you get caught short, suckered, I'm not going to shed a fucking tear. And if I go like a sucker, I don't want anybody, not any of you, shedding a tear over me."

If there weren't at least six of us covering Joey, it rattled some of the crew, even when he was staying close to home. About all he was doing was seeing the dentist in his apartment building, going to Mama Gallo's for dinner, and sometimes spending a couple of hours at Dolly's. That wasn't trouble. The problem was when he had to report to his parole officer over on Eighth and Fortieth in Manhattan. All the Colombos had to do was find out when and they'd be laying for him. Joey got his attorney uncle, Joe Iovine, to make different arrangements with his parole officer, switching around different days never announced in advance.

We were still even more worried that the other Families would come on us. Then I got a call from this particular individual from the Genovese crew, and I really worried.

A year and a half before, when we were still getting all the crap from Colombo, we considered swinging over with this Genovese crew. I was very tight with Vince Gigante, a capo, who we all called Chin, and through me Blast and Chin became very close friends. Chin was looking to put his arm around Blast and bring him in with his crew. Before doing that, he had to get the approval from Tommy Ryan,* who was running the Genovese Family.

Tommy Ryan ran hot and cold, liked us and

*Thomas Eboli.

didn't, and he wasn't all that sure Blast had the leadership of his crew, that it wouldn't be a problem when Joey came out of the can. But Chin was confident that Blast had control of his men.

The Genovese crew may have been having their own problems, or they wanted to strengthen themselves by adding ours. Once we were in with them, Chin was going to have some of us made. Blast said it would be me, Tony Bernardo, Punchy, and Roy-Roy. I could see Tony B, Punchy, and even Roy-Roy being made good fellows. "But me, Blast?" I'd asked him. "I'm no wop. You keep forgetting I'm Greek."

Blast hadn't forgotten, he said. He had it figured. He'd say my old man was a greaseball from Torre del Grecò, the Greek Tower, a town south of Naples, that after my old man died, my old lady, who it seemed was also Italian, remarried some Greek. I could just see the Council buying a full-blooded Greek as a greaseball. That would have been an insult. Blast thought things were changing.

"Not that much they're not," I said. I wasn't gullible enough to believe he was really serious.

Then when he went to see Joey and told him, Joey said to forget about it, that we weren't moving in with anybody, that Blast was not to make any moves until he got home. So Blast lost out on the only real chance he ever had to be made a good fellow. Colombo would never have made any one of us.

Now that Colombo had been clipped, Chin sent for us. This Gino called my apartment, and I called back on a safe phone. He wanted to set up an appointment with Blast and me at their club on Sullivan Street. He didn't want Joey in on this. He gave me some chill when he said it was about what happened at the banchetto and about that certain yahm.

That day, over at Dolly's, I told Blast. His eyes danced when he asked if I'd made the appointment.

"Not those kind of appointments, not until I talked to you."

"You tell Joey?"

"Nobody."

"Fine. Call Gino and see if you can set it up for

tonight. But nothing to nobody, particularly my brother."

This was the only thing I never told Joey. I called Gino from an outside booth. "Listen, sometime this evening." That was all I said.

He called right back. "Around nine. The club downtown. You know where. Vince will see you."

Blast was at the same table at Dolly's alone. "Well?"

"Around nine. Better get the pistols."

"No."

"What?"

"No hardware."

I looked at him. "You crazy? You want to go down there, no pieces, just you and me? Right now they could be loading up to clip us."

"It's meant to be, it'll be."

"Hey, I don't go with that thinking. It'll be turkey time."

"I know it."

"You know it? Come on, Blast. You value your life. I value mine. You can't think it's that important to go laundered and chance getting suckered."

"It's that important."

"Nothing's that important."

"We'll do it just like I said. We'll let somebody know."

"We'll let who know?"

"We'll let Pegleg know that we're going on an appointment, that we should be back in a couple of hours, and for him to stand by, not to leave the club until we come back."

"Yeah, we're going on an appointment. But don't you want to tell him who?"

"We'll tell him who, tell him where, and if we don't come back, he'll know who to tell."

"All right." I didn't like saying that at all.

Pegleg was Jimmy Springs,* an around guy. He'd lost his leg years before from gangrene. With his long mustache, peaked cap, and pipe, he looked like a sea

*James Connato.

captain. He was sitting by the window, watching the
street from the outside mirrors.

"Pegleg," I said, "come here." I whispered in his
ear and his eyes went wide. "Yeah," I said, "I know. I
don't like it either."

Gino was outside the club, waiting. When we
pulled up, he looked over the street before coming
over. He got in and started looking out the back window
before the car door even closed after him. I didn't
particularly care for it one bit with him being in back
of us.

"Thought we were going in," I said.

"No, Chin's apartment, Greek. I'll show you."

"Yeah," I said, moving the Caddy.

Blast had turned to him and asked, "How come
we're not meeting at the club or some restaurant?"

"Chin can't talk to you in the open. You're outlaws. You and the Greek with him, they'll figure a
conspiracy. Somebody makes you, we got to say what
we were doing with you, or we're sitting at the big table." Then he said, "Greek, better make some turns."

I'd already made the dusty black Plymouth in
back of us. I took one turn and it went straight. My
stomach was cold. With Gino behind us, it was a good
spot to shoot us both in the head. All the while Blast
sat with his arm over the top of his seat, talking to him,
but watching him all the time.

At apartment 4B Chin stood in the doorway, so
big he nearly filled all of it. He embraced Blast, then me,
kissing both of us, and offered us drinks, turning down
the TV. I sat where nobody could come up behind me,
trying to read both Chin and Gino. Gino was doing
the talking, smiling when he made small talk and still
smiling when he sat up in his chair, and said, "Now
the circle, Joe C getting whacked."

Just then there was a knock on the wall next door.
Chin got up, saying, "Excuse me." He went out, leaving
the door partly open. The blood pounded in me. I expected shooters to come in on us. I was ready to throw

everything I could. Blast cleared his throat, but his eyes were on the door.

Chin came in with that smile. "That's Frankie Ubatz next door. He's a nosy cocksucker. Wanted to know who just came in."

I tried to look into my glass of sherry.

Blast cleared his throat again. "You were saying."

"Yeah," said Chin, "about the circle. Well, certain people, myself included, don't know whether you did or you didn't whack out Joe C. And I'm telling you now, Blast, they're looking hard, they're investigating whether you did or you didn't. If you didn't, they need assurances. I need assurances."

"This gone to the table?" Blast asked.

"Just telling you certain people are very hot about the way it was done, with a yahm. Now if you guys get whacked out and you're innocent, it's only going to add to the whole shitting thing. These people need to be assured, and I myself feel that you and I have enough trust and faith in one another, and I hope to hear something so I can assure them."

"Chin," said Blast, "you want me to tell you we were looking to clip Colombo? We were. For three weeks solid we were looking. I can tell you how, I can tell you where, and I can tell you why, but you already know the reasons why."

"All right. Good. So where were you looking to clip him?"

Blast told him. Chin would nod or he'd smile, his forefinger resting on his cheek. Sometimes he'd interrupt and ask a question, and when it was answered right, he'd point his finger and say, "Good. Go on."

Blast told him our theories on who took off Colombo, including the one about Hoover. Chin smiled at that one. "Whose theory is *that?*" he asked.

"Punchy's. He even brought the CIA into it, which isn't worth commenting. Sure, Hoover was Colombo's biggest enemy, but he had a lot of other enemies. So who set it up? Was it Abby, who was being squeezed by Colombo for the greens, hating him but really hating us for taking off his old man? Did he work the Colombo hit so it would be thrown on us? Start a mob war by using a black? Was it Gambino, a way of shutting Colombo up? Was it Johnson on his own, some psychopath? Only a psychopath goes in, pulls a piece, and shoots, nothing prearranged. This was too premeditated. He poses as a news photographer, has the press pass. Anybody could have set him up with the fugazy, the phony press pass. But somebody big had to set him up. This guy wasn't on his own. So how was he convinced that he had strong backup, that he had the escape? It had to be somebody very big.

"We're *that* big to convince a guy? And you know we do our own work, not fancy shit like that. And even if we hired an out-of-town shooter, he'd be good, not some nut.

"I've really thought about it. Joey could never have worked this on his own, and I sure as hell wouldn't have gone along on something like this. What—to bring heat, to bring off a disgrace, to bring on animosity from all the different crews? Are we that stupid? It isn't our style, or anybody else's for that matter.

"It's like a Kennedy assassination. It's like this guy Johnson is from a different planet. If you think of the mob, it's Abby. He's the strongest possibility. But you know, and everybody else knows, that nobody has ever pulled off something like this. So who does it leave?"

Chin sat back, looking at both of us. "Well, you weren't about to have the Families come on you, the way it was done. I'm convinced of that. When I explain how you were going to make the comeoff, the right way, they'll also be convinced. You couldn't have worked the yahm like this."

"We never even thought about it," said Blast.

"Hey, I believe you." Then Chin asked if we wanted another drink. Blast said no, he was still working on his. I said I was fine. I could still feel my blood. I didn't know whether Chin really believed Blast or not. When he said the next thing, I knew he believed him, but I didn't like what was said.

"Well, now that Joe C's been whacked," he said, "and there's no real boss over there, I can tell you something which I could never mention before. And,

Blast, I'm telling you this because I want to reaffirm our friendship and faith in each other.

"Before Joey came out, Joe C approached me. Yeah. He wanted us to do the piece of work, to set you up—you and your brother."

"I had an inkling," said Blast.

"Joe C knew we were friends, that if I ever sent for you, you'd come. He knew that once Joey hit the streets, he was going to move a lot of shit around, and he was right. Well, it was up to me to say yes or no. I said no. He still wanted to whack you out. So you guys weren't so stupid moving on him."

Afterward Blast and I headed down in the elevator. We were both reading each other's eyes. He said, "Did you feel it?"

"Feel it? Thought we had it."

"The most uncomfortable feeling I've ever had in my life."

"What's this you had an inkling?"

"A guy in Chin's crew—he sort of hinted, saying to be careful."

"When?"

"Week before Joey came home."

"And you knew this?"

"I knew it. Knew Chin wasn't going to come on Joey and me now that I'd been told."

"Hey, if you had told me this before we went, I wouldn't have gone with my fucking finger. I wouldn't have gone at all unless we had five guys packing, and I mean packing. You knew this and you got me and yourself going in there, in an apartment where they could have really taken us off without any problems?"

"Know what you're thinking."

"You know? I'm glad you know."

"At least be glad we're still alive."

"We're not out of here yet," I said.

Outside, I checked real good to see if anybody was on the block or laying in the back seat of the car. After we drove off I thought to myself, here's Blast, a smart guy, doing some dumb shit like this, going for all that greaseball faith and trust crap, and the guy was looking to take him and Joey off, and maybe was looking to take both of us off now. Thought we had it when Chin left the door open. Maybe Colombo shooters were waiting with shotguns and Chin telling them to cool it. Some deep friendship he had with Blast, all right, some honor and respect.

We had gone several blocks before Blast reminded me, "This is never to be revealed to Joey or anyone. And I mean no one."

"Yeah, Blast."

"Feel worse now. We were being set up."

"Now you know it."

"Feel very uncomfortable about the whole thing."

"Yeah, Blast. Very, very uncomfortable," I said.

eight

Nearing my apartment one night, I checked the street, which was lit with all those yellow high-intensity lights. I saw no one, just parked cars. I drove around a second time before I parked by the hydrant right across from the house.

My wife was watching from the top terrace. She waved that it was clear. I laid my jacket over my arm, covering the piece, cocked and ready to go. I started across the street when a car came along. I doubled back around my car as a grubby dark Ford stopped and double-parked in front of the entrance way. Two guys got out and went into the vestibule, one unlocking the inside door with a key. I'd never seen either one of them before.

I watched them head for the elevator and go up. I went in and checked the lobby. The elevator lights showed they had stopped on the sixth, my floor. Then the elevator stopped on the fifth. Now it was coming all the way down. I hadn't touched the button. The electric whine slowed as it started to settle. I moved to one side and slid back twenty feet. The door bucked, then opened. It was only some woman with an older lady. The younger one seemed a little wary, while the other jerked her chin going by.

Before the elevator door closed, I put the key that the super had given me into the panel, locking out all the other floors. On the sixth I held the door part way open with my foot, sticking my head and pistol out to look. Instead of shooters, I saw my wife carrying the baby.

The baby, Laura, three and a half, wasn't all that small. Kitty was swayed backward, having a time with her draped over her shoulder. Laura was asleep, her arms hanging straight.

"Oh, my Christ," I said.

"It's all right, Pete. It's all right."

"Kitty, the baby."

"She heard the phone. You know how she is."

"Get her inside."

She went in ahead of me. In the living room the TV was on with the eleven o'clock news. Kitty, watching me, sat down on the sofa, still holding the baby. I couldn't look at her when I said, "I never want you to do that again."

She was rocking her a little. "I'll get her to bed."

I sat watching the TV, not seeing anything. When she came down the stairs, she sat at the end of the sofa. I kept watching the dumb TV.

"Pete, you're angry."

"No, not angry."

"Know you are when you hold your chin up like that."

"Jesus Christ, the baby."

"She heard the phone, really she did."

"Kitty."

"She came down asking if that was you. I told her to get straight back to bed. But she said, 'No, I want to see Daddy.' You know how she is. Just wouldn't go back to bed. What else could I do?"

"She was asleep. You saw those two guys, didn't you?"

She looked away, her hand going to her face.

"What did you figure?" I asked. "Figured maybe

they're not just visiting? Figured maybe they were going on me when they got off the sixth, that they'd take me from the stairwell when I came out of the elevator? Sure, that's how you figured. And what did you do then? Check the stairwells? And if they were who you thought they were, what do you think would have happened with you coming in on them and they got pistols out? Did you think of that? My Christ. And you with the baby. The baby, Kitty."

She took hold of me then, trembling all through her. "No," she said. "They wouldn't have. They wouldn't have done anything." She was really shaking her head against me. "No, not me, not the baby."

I had bad chills in the elevator. Now I had different chills. Those two could have been laying to take me off, laying in either stairwell, and with the hall straight, the elevator in the center of the floor—turkey time. But with Kitty and Laura in the middle of that? My good Christ.

Ever since Colombo had taken the shot, she was shaky whenever I came home and whenever I had to leave. She'd see me with the binoculars checking the street. Well, I had to think about a lot of things, and she knew it too. Then if Bobby Darrow or a couple of the guys weren't coming around to pick me up, I'd have to chance it on my own. That was when it really got scary for her.

Whenever I'd lay up in the apartment, I'd phone Dolly's, say I was home, and wait. Sometimes Blast, only down the end of the hall, would call for someone to pick him up. You knew that at least two cars would come to get him, and the stairwells and everything would be checked with walkie-talkies. You didn't have to worry too much with all that was happening. And it was the same coming back.

It was another matter coming back on your own. I would never drive down the ramp into the apartment's garage. Even with the electric eye triggering open the big door, and your hand right on the pistol, they could be laying for you when the door swung open, or when you went down the next day to get the car.

I'd call Kitty, but tell her only where I was calling from. She knew just how long it would take me to get home. You didn't know if the law, who had a tap on the phone, was peddling information back to the Colombos. So I'd just say where I was calling from, and she knew that it really meant I was leaving.

I'd come out either on the sixth or seventh floor. At least with the duplex I could come in either way —through the bedrooms on the seventh or the living room on the sixth. It wasn't so easy for a couple of guys to lay on the stairwell if they couldn't be sure what floor I'd be using.

Still, the stairwells worried me. So did the elevator and everything else. But it worried Kitty a lot more, and when she knew I was coming home, she'd sometimes stay up half the night waiting for my call, then go out on the terrace to see if everything was clear and give me the sign.

The only time she relaxed, or seemed to, was when I laid up. She was never one for asking questions, but after Colombo was clipped, she began talking about what was coming over the TV or what was in the papers, mainly that we were behind this Jerome Johnson. Once I asked her, "Really think, babe, that we had anything to do with it, or that I did?" She said nothing. I told her the less she knew about that the better. If she ever got hauled before a grand jury, she could only tell the truth, which was exactly nothing. I don't suppose that helped her believe that we had nothing to do with it.

The other thing was the business of all the blacks that came down to Blast and Papa Gallo while Joey was in the slams, and came around after Joey came home. The papers had made it sound as though Joey had recruited a black army of militants or had started a black Mafia. I never told her much about that, except to ask if she'd ever seen a black army on President Street. The papers were full of it, as usual.

Sometimes she'd ask funny questions. One was why they called Albert Kid Blast. That was a funny question coming from her, something she had never once asked. Now she wanted to know everything.

She was loading up the dishwasher and I was sitting at the kitchen table, waiting for the coffee to perk. "Why do they?" she asked.

I didn't answer her right off. I said that was a funny question, but I told her anyway. When Blast was a young kid, he was something of a casanova, and whenever he'd come back from this or that broad, we'd ask if he blasted her. I made the motion, pumping my fist.

"That's why?" she said.

"That's why. That's how he got the name of Kid Blast. It's not for what everyone thinks it means, a pistolero."

She began talking about how I should stay away from the house as much as possible, for my own sake. When I asked where she wanted me to go, I saw her eyes go differently. She wasn't one to take a gummare thrown in her face, but she must have known I had one.

Then she began talking about my getting out of the crew, and that too was something she'd never once talked about. She wanted us to move away, get the kids away, anything. It just wasn't like her to talk about things like that. All I'd say was, "I can't, that's all." I knew she wanted to go further with that, yet she wouldn't say anything else.

After what had happened with her and the baby, I got her to take some sherry, then had her go to bed. She was hanging onto me in the bed. I had one arm around her. I kept looking up at the dark ceiling, wondering how she could love me that much. I mean, who would put her own kid up for the shot? What woman would do that for her man? I thought about it for a long time.

One Saturday I was sitting around in my house slippers and robe, reading the papers, trying to keep the kids quiet, when I heard Kitty. I asked, "What?"

"I said it's beautiful out."

"Yeah, it's beautiful."

"It's going to really be a warm, beautiful day."

"The sun's strong, all right. It'll be hot."

"Why don't we all go to Brighton and go swimming?"

"Babe, you know I can't, not with you and the kids."

Later the phone rang. It was Roy-Roy Musico at Dolly's, telling me to come down.

Kitty watched me heading upstairs for the bedroom. "Are they coming for Albert?"

"Nobody's coming for Blast."

"Pete, who called?"

"Roy-Roy."

"Bobby coming?"

"Nobody."

After I dressed, I went to the window, taking the binoculars out of the case. The sun was hot, glaring, reflecting bright flashes off cars passing, hurting your eyes. People were out, nobody to worry about, just Jewish ladies sitting around on beach chairs, taking the sun. It was some nice day. Then I heard Kitty say, "Pete? All right to come in?"

I wound up the strap on the binocular case, put it back in the drawer, and made sure there was nothing she could see before I opened the door. Kitty and all the kids came in. My son, Ray, was complaining that nobody let him watch the TV program he always watched. Laura was hugging me around the leg. Then my older daughter wanted to know why I never went anywhere with them anymore. I told Kitty, "I have to go."

Kitty said, "Kids, get downstairs. Have to talk to your father."

They ah-ed about that, but they went. Laura was still holding onto me. I said, "Get her downstairs."

Kitty's eyes were a little wide as she took the baby behind her. "I've thought and thought about it, and it's the only sensible thing to do."

"Don't say it. I don't want to hear it."

"You don't even know what I want to say."

"I know what you want to say."

"Nothing'll happen if we're with you."

"Look, you're not coming down with me." I gave her something of a kiss, the baby too. I had the door open, then closed it right behind me before they had a chance to come out after me. I checked both stairwells, the pistol cocked and ready. I was waiting for the elevator when Kitty came along with Laura. They were both walking fast. "That's as far as you go." I was almost yelling.

"No," she said. "We're going down with you."

I gave one yell, "Get back inside!" They both stopped.

Downstairs, the only time I really looked around was when I got to the vestibule, checking the street again. The car looked all right. The Jewish ladies, all sitting in a line of beach chairs, missed nothing. When I got behind the wheel, I tapped into the bumper of the car in front. I looked back when I made the corner. Kitty and the baby were standing out on the terrace, watching me.

That night it rained. With Bobby Darrow, I picked up some vig money in Greek Town on Eighth Avenue in lower Manhattan, that's jammed with coffee houses and tavernas. I left the car parked, and looked for a taxi. Everything was shiny in the rain. The rain made everything worse.

I hailed a cab. It smelled of wet plastic. Inside it was hot and stuffy with the bullet-proof partition closed between us and the driver. Bobby wanted another cab. The partition made him uncomfortable. The driver cocked his ear. I told him, "Just head up Eighth."

He shook his head, cupping his ear. "Didn't get you."

"Can't you hear?" asked Bobby. "It's them god-damned partitions. He said head up Eighth."

Bobby sat back. He was complaining that the rain had messed up his suit. He didn't like anything happening to his clothes. He looked the way he always did, snappy and dark and mean. Now he was especially mean, complaining about the partition again, that it made you feel like you were in the can. He was sweating, opening his window further than the decal sticker said to, forcing it. "So where the fuck we headed?"

"Don't know. Feel like bouncing."

"Seeing your gummare tonight?"

"Maybe. Yeah, maybe I will. Maybe for a week I'll see her."

"You're in some shitty mood," he said, slapping the partition. "Why do they have to have them fucking things anyway?" He yelled to the driver, "Think they'll protect you?"

"What?"

He rapped with his knuckles. "This fucking thing."

"Supposed to."

"Yeah? With a three-fifty-seven mag, pal, it'll go through *it,* you, and the engine block. It's stupid having them, and making everybody damned uncomfortable."

"How far you fellas want to go?"

"Not too goddamned far. I'm cooking."

"I'll let you know," I said. Then to Bobby, "Stop breaking balls."

We stopped for a light. Traffic was heavy. We hadn't even made Thirty-fourth Street. It was hot, all right. The driver straightened up something alongside his seat, then took his clipboard, writing on it. A colored broad, her hand out, was standing off the curb, trying to hail a cab, holding an umbrella that was more like a parasol with plastic flowers. She had some shape to her. Bobby came alive. "Va-va-cum," he said. "Would I like to shaft her."

The driver looked at us in the rear-view mirror. "Wouldn't pick up a nigger if you paid me. Wouldn't if she was with John Lindsay and Sammy Davis, Jr."

"Hey, gumba," Bobby said to the driver, "know what a white nigger is? That's a wop turned inside out. We're white niggers."

The driver took a good look at us in the mirror, then closed the slot in the partition. Bobby said he felt like rapping the sonofabitch. I told him he always felt like rapping somebody, and someday somebody was going to blow him away. He sat back with that jittery way of his.

A green panel truck passed us, one like we had used. Bobby snickered. "Know what I see, Greek? Apples out on the porch of the funeral parlor."

My forefinger went to my lips.

"Fuck, he can't hear." Then, smiling, he said, "Had him good. Had him real good. I wouldn't have fucked up like I did."

He was talking about the time he clipped Apples McIntosh. The Persico crew and ours had been part of the Colombo Family, but the old grievances were there, and when Bobby and Louis P, a Gambino, went into their ginmill, where they had no business, Junior's brother Allie Boy* and Jerry Lang† started to abuse them. Then Apples got into it, slapping the both of them. They took a step back and left, went right to where they'd stashed the pistols, and came back.

It was well after closing, but the Persicos were still inside. Instead of waiting for them to come out—the right way—the two went up to the door and knocked. When the owner saw them over the top of the café curtain, he said, "We're closed. Get out of here." Then it was Apples looking over the top of the curtain, asking, "What the fuck you want now?" Both Bobby and Louis had their pistols leveled right at his belly. "*This!*" yelled Bobby, and both of them emptied out, saw Apples go down, and figured they'd killed him good.

Apples was taken to Coney Island Hospital. He told the law that a car had come by, that he hadn't seen who shot him.

That had to go before the table, the sitdown. Apples was known to be mean and abusive when he drank, and it didn't go too good for him being only half Italian when Bobby and Louie P were all Italian. Besides Louie P was a Gambino under Frankie Blair's‡ crew. That also made a difference. Apples lost the decision.

The cab lurched and stopped short.

Bobby, fanning himself, said, "Where the hell *are* we going?"

"How do I know? Just going."

"But you know that you're going with your gum-

*Alphonse Persico.
†Jerry Langella.
‡Francesco Smurra.

mare after, huh? When you got a wife like Kitty?"

"Knock off that shit. Get off me."

"If I had a wife like Kitty, I wouldn't be going with—"

I threw a hook, giving him some belt. His head bounced against the padded seat like a speed bag.

He held his ear, staring at me. "Why'd you bust me?"

"Told you to get off me."

"What the fuck did I say?"

"Nothing, not a goddamned thing."

We were in midtown. The rain kept coming down. I guess it made everybody miserable.

nine

I awoke when the phone rang, seeing a silk flowered sleeve passing over my face. Edith Russo, my gummare, was reaching for the receiver. She sat up on her knees on the bed, shaking back her long hair to take the phone to her ear. "Hello," she said, then looked at me, passing it over.

"It's me, Greek." It was Bobby Darrow. Then his voice became very low. "Why'd you bust me last night?"

I could still see him leaving the cab, when we got to midtown, saying, "Fuck you," and going off with that hop of his when he was sauced, that way he tilted to one side.

"You still with that?" I asked.

"Tell me."

"I'll tell you."

"Yeah, tell me."

I looked at Edith. "Go in the other room a minute." When she'd gone, I told Bobby, "Listen, you fuck, when you're tanked, you're not only nasty, you're nosy. My personal business is my business. You don't cross over from my wife to my gummare. Understood?"

"So what did I say?"

"You said enough. You talked about my wife."

"Must have been stoned. Hey, some ear you gave me, pal. I can hang a wine barrel off it."

"You coming up?"

"That's why I'm calling."

"Check with Joey?"

"Another reason I'm calling. He's not at the house. He's no place."

"What?"

"Went for a walk, by himself."

I threw the sheet off me, sitting up. "Better get up here."

When Edith heard me rack the phone, she asked, "What's wrong?"

"Plenty," I said, dialing Joey's number. First his daughter answered; then his wife came on. I asked her where he was.

"He's taking a walk."

"A walk? Where?" I was already getting my pants on. "How long has this been going on?"

"Couple of days. He's got me worried."

"He's got *you* worried?"

"Maybe he's only getting the papers."

"Only the papers? Maybe he wants to make the papers. He comes in, tell him we're on our way, to wait there."

Bobby came up inside of ten minutes. When we got over to Joey's apartment he was sitting, reading the papers, having his coffee, giving me one of those sidelong glances of his and that half-smile, the mole on his cheek making a jump, when I said, "Good morning, Mr. Joseph Gallo. Had your little morning constitutional I see, like Mr. Fucking Harry Truman. Mr. Harry S. Fucking Truman."

"Yeah, Greek."

"And would you mind very much telling me where, Mr. Gallo?"

"Get off that Mr. Gallo shit."

"Sure. Get off taking walks by yourself." I sat down on the sofa, taking a coffee cup, looking at him all the time, passing a cup to Bobby. "Do you have your coffee spiked with a little anisette? Well, pal, put a lot in ours. You had both of us going." I looked to see if Jeffie and the kid were around, then I waved my hand, saying, "Where the fuck do you come off taking walks by yourself? You want to walk? Good, but take somebody with you."

He patted my stomach. "It would do you a lot of good, Greek."

"So where'd you go?"

"No place. Just around."

"Oh, around."

"Nice out."

"Oh, very nice out. Very nice you're not laying out there."

It was sticking to the apartment that got to him. He'd done too many years in the slams, and now that we'd tightened up he found himself in another. He had missed out on too many things, and he wanted to catch up on all of it. So after that Bobby Darrow and I would go walking with him around Greenwich Village. He enjoyed the streets in the summer, enjoyed everything, even those oil paintings in the windows—on black velvet some of them—or the stores with wicker baskets hanging out front, the coffeehouses with straightback chairs and small tables outside. Most of all he liked looking at the broads. He'd see one and, fast, his hand would jab you on the shoulder. "Greek, Greek," he'd say. "Look at *that* one. Mamma mìa. Look at those boobies bouncing."

There he'd be in a sports shirt, the old-style pants with cuffs, his peaked cap and sunglasses, and he'd be taking in everything. Liked the broads especially when they were braless. He'd feel like nuzzling them right then and there, or he'd say there ought to be a law. He was bowled over with the way things were now.

Well, it was all different, like his fucking pants were different, and I'd ask him when was he going to get with it. He'd say, "Don't give me none of that jive talk, Greek."

After that he got pants with no cuffs, conservative bell bottoms. He said he had to get used to them, that he had to get used to a lot of things and didn't know if he had the time left to catch up on everything he'd missed out on. But he really felt good about everything, loving the Village and telling you how much he hated the lowlifes on Times Square, that the Village was where the real life was. Sometimes I wondered if he saw something I didn't, but I sure as hell didn't appreciate getting up that early in the morning just to walk around.

Whenever Joey came down to President Street or we went over to his mother's or down to Cellini Furniture, where he had to make a showing for his parole since he was supposed to be a salesman there, the law would be on us heavy. So instead of worrying about a roust, their coming down and finding pistols, we had Cousin Tony come along with us for the first couple of weeks. He had the permit, since he was a disabled ex-fireman, and packed a three-fifty-seven magnum and some other piece. At least we had something to grab, had half a chance, and with the law hanging on our tail it was even better.

Joey would give the cops hand signals to show them the way we were headed. When we were stuck in traffic, he'd yell, "Stick close, fellas," and maybe even go over to them and tell them which way we were going. They loved that, all right. Well, we needed the extra protection. Nice, since we didn't have to pay for it besides.

You never knew what he was going to do next. When his nephew Stevie Gallo got pinched by the federal narcs, Joey went the next morning to his arraignment. He stood up, telling the judge Stevie was a good boy. The judge told him to sit down. Later I asked if he was playing a Clarence Darrow over there. He could have gotten himself into a swindle. He said Stevie was a good boy. I said, "Yeah, when he sleeps. He's the best."

Another time that summer he called Bobby Darrow late one morning, telling him to come right over and pick him up. When Bobby called and told me, I told him to wait, but Joey didn't want to wait for anybody. Bobby was only a block away and Joey didn't want to take the time to wait for me to come all the way from Ocean Parkway—exactly what the Colombos were waiting for him to do.

Bobby said they'd be by Dolly's no later than one-thirty. If Joey said he'd be by at a certain time, he always was. This time, though, he didn't show until after five. Joey said they'd stopped for a cup of coffee. I asked if they drank the whole fifty-gallon urn. Then Joey and Blast went to the back tables.

Bobby Darrow told me they'd been over to Sullivan Street.

"Who'd you see?"

"Chin."

"What?"

"I never want to go over there again," he said.

A week before, Bobby Darrow had heard about the meet with Chin, probably from Pegleg. He'd wanted to know, and I had said it was better he didn't. He kept on about it, saying he was my partner, that we never kept anything from each other. So I told him and explained that if he ever yapped about it, Blast would turn on the big freeze and Joey would be very, very pissed that we had been so stupid.

Now I was concerned that he had told Joey. He assured me and swore on his mother that he hadn't, that Joey just wanted to go down there and talk to his old friend.

We were at a table where nobody could hear us, and I said, "You'd better tell me everything."

"Listen, you know him. He decides to go, you go."

"Tell me exactly, and I mean exactly."

"Well, we pulled on the block. Gino, outside, saw me get out, saw Joey get out. We were like double-parked. Gino jumped in, said he'd take the car from there. So we go inside. Soon as Chin saw him, they did with the grabbing, like they both loved each other. Then Chin had them lock the doors, close the curtains, and put two guys outside. So like I'm supposed to, with all this fucking respect, I indicate to Chin that I got a pistol on me.

" 'Quite all right,' he says, 'Keep it on.'

" 'I just want to let you know,' I says.

" 'Quite all right,' he says. 'I know why you got it on. I know you didn't come here to do anything with that toward us. If you want, we can stash it for you. Take it with you when you leave.'

"I figure I did the right thing. I look at Joey, and he gives me that stiff nod of his to give it to him. So I give him the pistol and he has them put it away."

"So how'd you feel?"

"Forget about it. When I gave up that pistol, I felt like we gave up our lives. Felt like we were never going to get out of there, especially when they closed the curtains and locked the doors, put the guys outside. Hey, pal, I got the fucking cagetta."

"Now you know how it feels."

"Never going down there again. You can believe that."

That evening, driving Joey home, I asked him, "Whatever made you go down to Sullivan Street? Just to say hello?"

"What the fuck, Greek. I'm just out of the can, and I want to say hello to some of my old friends."

"You mean you really wanted to get certain vibes, if they're still your friends, or who your friends *really* are."

"What're you looking at me like that for, Greek?"

"What do you mean, I'm looking? I'm not looking at you. I'm looking at the fucking road. I'm driving."

"Yeah, but that one fucking eye is looking at me pretty good."

"Maybe now you know if they're coming on us. So are they?"

"They know pretty good that we had nothing to do with Mr. Joe C, like they had a direct fucking line. Curious isn't it?"

"Yeah," I said. "Guess it is."

After we got him home I asked Bobby, "You sure you didn't tell Joey anything?"

He swore on all the saints, his mother, and a lot of other things that he hadn't. I believed him. But I was sure that Joey hadn't gone just for a cup of coffee and a talk with old friends.

ten

A while back two of our bookies were out over forty-five grand that a guy in Joey Gambino's crew owed them. Blast, myself, and Bobby Darrow went up to this wiseguy club in Westchester. Joey G, a capo, was Carlo Gambino's cousin. He and Skinny Phil, a good fellow, were at a table talking to this guy named Nick who was going away to do some time in the slams.

We waited at the round bar. I eyed the whole place and them. I'd never met Joey Gambino before. He was one natty dresser, but with his four-carat diamond pinky ring and a diamond tie tack even bigger, he was shining like a big neon. Skinny Phil wasn't nearly as sharp. For at least a half-hour they talked. Then, after this Nick left, Gambino—as small as his cousin Carlo—went over to the kitchen while Skinny Phil came over to the bar to tell us the meet was downstairs.

"Downstairs where?" It just came out of me.

"The cellar."

The three of us looked at each other. What kind of greaseball tactic was this? Either they're trying to

psyche us out or shoot us. I was waiting for Blast to
say something. If it was my place, I would have.

"Ah, *scusate*," said Skinny Phil. "Reason we wanna go down to the cellar is because we no wanna nobody see us talk and make you over here."

It was all right for them to talk to that Nick who
was going away to do some time, but they didn't want to
talk in the open with us. And there we were, nothing
on us and heading down to the cellar.

At the first flight was a big shepherd chained,
showing his teeth. Skinny Phil said not to worry. "He's
a nice dog, only growl." Then we went down another
flight of steps, so dark we couldn't see each other.
When Skinny Phil found the light, he saw us all dis-
persed—me in the middle, Blast way to the left, Darrow all the way to the right.

Skinny Phil brought his hands together, like he
was praying, waving them. "*Mama-ru-gam*," he went,
thinking he was up for the hit.

The basement was another dining room. When
Joey Gambino came in, glasses were set up with bottles of wine and scotch, and after Skinny Phil made
the introduction Joey Gambino toasted us with a
"*scindone*," tapping all the glasses. He had a worse
accent than Skinny Phil. Then we got down to business.

Blast talked about it for quite a while, and Joey
Gambino would say "Hokay" to this and "Hokay" to
that, that he hadda getta back to hissa man, no bigga
problem. Blast suggested we get the two bookies and
Gambino's man together for a meet, have all the figures, and work out some sort of arrangement. Gambino said, "Hokay," shook hands with Blast, then with
us, and then more or less apologized for the manner of
the meet.

We met a few times after that and set up a meet in
a restaurant with the two bookies and Gambino's guy.
The figure settled was fifteen thousand. The bookmakers weren't very happy.

Months went by. Joey came home. Then I heard
Skinny Phil had gone up to this place in Fishkill, New

York, and had given this kid a few slaps since he was owed something like four thou. What Phil didn't know was that I was partners with the kid in an Italian egg-roll business. So Phil and I had to have a talk.

At a restaurant Skinny Phil, a napkin tucked into his shirt, got up and shook hands, and after we sat down and I ordered, he said, "I don't know you involved with that kid over there. That kid owes me money."

"He owes you money? He owes me money. I'm involved over there."

"Ah, *scusate*. I don't know you involved."

"Still makes no difference. Listen, the guy disrespected you? You give him a *motsada*,* that's all."

"Hey, I don't do that now I know you involved. We straighten it out."

"Of course, we can straighten it out."

"Ah, but Joey Gambino involved with the kid over there."

"Wait a while. You making a claim for the kid— that the business is yours?"

"No, no, no. Making no claim."

"As long as you're not making a claim, we can talk. But if you're making a claim, then we'll have to have a sitdown. We'll talk differently. I'm here because the kid is concerned, and I don't want anything to happen to him."

"No, no, no. Forget. Call him, tell him ever'thing all right. Okay? Long as you are involved, we straighten it out. Now you finish your eat, huh? The calamari is very good," he said.

They didn't get their money, and the kid was tapping me besides, writing all kinds of checks until the business went bust. Then, four weeks after Colombo was clipped, Skinny Phil called about the money. This time Joey Gambino wanted to see me. I'd know where. I figured it was more than the money they were calling about.

Over at Dolly's we were talking about my going to the club in Westchester for this meet with Carlo Gam-

*A backhanded slap.

bino's cousin and Skinny Phil when Joey asked, "Those the guys that had you go down in the cellar? Well, I'll tell you how you're going this time. You take four fucking pistoleros with you, you and Darrow—that's six. You two go in first, and you talk. Gambino says the cellar, you tell him, '*Walyo, aspet uno minuto. We're carrying and we got four guys outside with pistols.*' Indicate ahead of time that you're packing for reasons you don't have to explain."

"Joey, I know all this," I said.

"All right, but that's the way you're going. He tells you the cellar, you tell Darrow to bring in the other four guys. You see a shadow, shoot, then shoot him, and then we'll straighten everything out afterward. Not one of my fucking men, at no fucking given time, is going to go greaseball style and sit down in a fucking basement. They want to talk, they talk a different meet, in the open."

"That's the way you want it? Don't worry. It'll be taken care of. Anything moves down there, anything at all, we shoot it, him and Skinny Phil too. Okay?"

"Yeah, Greek," he said, grinning. "Go 'head. Go do your shit."

I went in the back, and there was the Mod Squad blowing pot. I waved the stink away, rounding up Joey's nephew Stevie Gallo, Bulleye, and Stevie Cirillo. Bobby Boriello was at an outside table with some of the guys. I was considering taking him as a fourth when Joey said, "Never mind Bullshit Bob."

Bobby Boriello was coming up with excuses now that Joey was the hot number one. He hadn't shown up the night before to cover Joey, giving the usual that he was sick.

"Come here, Bullshit," he said to Boriello. As big and lanky as Bobby Boriello was, he went lankier. Joey took him by his shirt, pulling him over the table. "What's this bullshit, Bullshit, you're giving me all the time?"

Boriello's neck was down to his shoulders. "But, Joey, I was sick. Had a bad cold. Still got it."

" 'Still got it'," he mimicked. "Scared shit you got, Bullshit. When I want you down, you come up with excuses, kid excuses. 'Teacher, may I go home now? My stomach don't feel so good, and my nose is running.' Bullshit, your ass is running."

"Joey, honest."

"Honest?" He pulled a piece. *"This* is honest." He shoved the barrel right under his jawbone, pushing back his head. "Now ask teacher if I should blow your fucking head off."

"Joey, don't," Bobby said, his eyes wide and blinking, trying to work his mouth, then closing his eyes tight.

Joey shoved him off the table, firing six rounds, right into the telephone booth. Bobby went under the table, scrambling. Blast didn't like that at all. The booth was shot up good. Somebody said that was one way of getting back at Ma Bell.

The law was on the block but nobody came in on us. Even if they had, they only would have asked whose car had backfired, or maybe said the appearance of the telephone booth was improved. That's the way it was on President Street.

I didn't think Bobby Boriello would come up with anymore kid excuses after that. I was sure of that. Still, I didn't take him with us to Westchester.

Outside the club I briefed them again. Bulleye listened, his big eyes dancing behind those thick glasses. They seemed to go three times their size. "Bulleye," I said, "you're not too good a shot. Be careful. We don't want to shoot each other. If we do, that fucking Jimmy Breslin will really get his rocks off.

Bobby Darrow and I went in. Skinny Phil greeted us, taking us over to the round bar while Joey Gambino spoke to some people. Afterward he came over, shaking hands. "Holloa, Pete. Nicea to see you. How ever'thing?"

"Fine. How's everything with you?"

"Hokay. Wella as canna be expect."

He pointed his finger to the bartender to set up drinks. When the bartender moved off, I said, "Listen, I'm packing. We're both packing."

"I canna well un'erstan'."

"I don't want to bring no heat to your place. And not only are we packing, but we got three guys in the car packing also."

If he had any ideas about the cellar, he changed his mind when he sat down.

"Pertaining to the money the kid owes you here," I said, "you know the business went bust. But I'm having him sell the equipment. It'll bring more than the money he owes both of us, and I'll make sure you get your money."

"Hey, I appreciater thata very much, Pete. Likea to breakin his fuckina facea."

"You want to break his face? I want to break his face. But we're not going to get our money that way. All we'll get is subpoenas to the grand jury."

"Hey, youa righta, one hun'red percent. So whatta we gonna do?"

"What we're going to do is sell the stuff and get our money. I'm concerned that you get yours."

Afterward he said, "Wanna thanka you very mucha comin' up special, with things so hot for you righta now, and things are happen becauser Joe Colombo."

I saw how he looked at me then.

"Hope you don't think we had anything to do with that."

"Ah, nah. Whatsamatter for you? Know better you guyser got nuttin' to do with dat."

"Just wanted you to understand that we absolutely had nothing—"

"I capisci."

"As long as you understand."

"I un'erstan'. My cousiner too, Carlo Gambino. Thisa guy, Joe Colombo, on the bandwagons, makea with the mouther, television, likea big actor, and my cousiner tella him, 'Walyo, get offa the bandwagons.'"

"I really appreciate that your cousin understands and you understand."

"I un'erstan', Pete. You no haver to explain to me. That Colombo fuckiner assahole anyway."

"Good, I'm glad that you're saying it, and I'm hearing it from you."

"Ah, sure."

"And I hope you don't feel offended that we came in here with pistols."

"No, no. I *capisci*. I un'erstan'. An' no worry. Have another drinka with me."

"Thank you, we will."

We had a drink, wished him well, said good night, and offered our best regards to his cousin.

"Ah, sure. Definate, by alla means."

"If there's anything we can do at any time, don't hesitate to call me."

"I appreciate that very mucha, Pete, that you leaver that way—nice."

"Thank you." And I said good night again.

eleven

We'd made our rounds in Greek Town one night, then stopped at the Port Said, when Little Freddy* came over to the bar, just standing alongside. He wouldn't look at us. He still had those bruises and scratches on his jaw. Bobby Darrow moved all the way to the other end of the bar.

"Freddy," I said, "who told you we were here?"

"Just left Joey," he said, still not looking at anyone. He seemed as though everything had gone out of him.

I said, "Let's get a table."

He was one of the around guys of our crew. He was so small, I don't think he came to five foot. Like most little guys who had to make up for something, he'd really get nasty when he was drunk. Once, in an afterhours joint, he took a swing at a guy who was so big that Freddy had to jump up in the air, only the big guy just leaned back. Freddy caught a lot of air. Then

*Fred Loporte.

95

the guy took him by the neck and seat of his pants and was about to throw him across the bar. I had to deck the guy. Little Freddy was always getting himself into something.

The last time, at Sammy the Syrian's bar, had been too much for everybody. Little Freddy made the mistake of taking on Bobby Boriello, who had more than a foot on him. It wasn't over anything at all, and Little Freddy went on him. Bobby B, more surprised than anything, started throwing punches, and when the guys tried to break it up Boriello went crazy, vaulting the bar, going for Sammy's pistol, screaming he was going to kill him.

I was on him before he got the pistol out of the cigar box, yelling if he wanted to kill somebody, kill some Colombo, while Stevie Boriello, Bobby's brother, just as big, was going on Little Freddy, and I was yelling, "We killing each other now?" Then a couple more of the guys started going on Freddy, like they'd been saving it, letting it go all at once.

A couple of us were trying to break it up. I got Freddy around the waist, and he was jumping like a bouncing spring, yelling, "I'll kill them! I'll kill them!" I had him off his feet, getting him into my car, and I was yelling, "There's four of them! You're going to kill all of them?"

I got him in the car, all right. Guys were coming out of the bar after him, with other guys trying to stop them, when I drove off. Little Freddy was still yelling that he'd kill them. Then, as though he finally realized that I had him in the car, he asked, "Where you taking me?"

"Taking you for a ride, that's all, till you cool off."

He stared at me. Then, "Turn that key! Stop this fucking car!"

"Whatsamatter with you?"

I was coming to an intersection, slowing for the light, when he reached over to turn the ignition off. I shoved him clear across the seat. He was out the door, yelling, "You're not! You're not!" He jumped, almost sprawling over, running right for all the cars, nearly

getting clipped by one when it swerved around him. He
just kept running.

Afterward he told everyone that I was out to shoot
him dead. When Joey heard about it, he said Freddy
wasn't only nasty and surly when he drank, he was
paranoid. And all the laying around, waiting for something to happen, was weighing on everybody. He had to
do something about Freddy.

He sent for him, telling him that the crew was uptight enough without Freddy causing dissension and
having his men fighting among themselves, that it was
something he would never tolerate. Then he told him
maybe he shouldn't come around for a while, asked if
he had some money, and gave him a couple of hundred
to travel.

Now, at the table of the Port Said, Freddy was telling me about it, saying he felt bad, real bad. He
would have felt a lot worse if the kid, Bobby Boriello,
had shot him. Then I asked, "So where you going?"

"Don't know. Maybe California. Don't know
yet." Then he was sorry that he thought I was going to
shoot him.

"Hey, there isn't a bullet small enough for that."

"Had it in my head, that's all. You've shot a lot of
guys."

"Yeah?"

"Yeah, Greek. Yeah."

We talked a while, then he had to get going. I told
him maybe it was for the best. The bad stuff was yet to
come. He said he felt real lousy. We shook hands, and
I wished him luck. He said, "Yeah, Greek. You too.
You're going to need it."

After he'd gone, Bobby Darrow came over. "What
was that all about?"

"Joey chased him."

"Good. We don't need any of that shit." Then,
"Whatsamatter, Greek?"

"What do you think's the matter? We haven't
made a decent score in months."

"Maybe we'll take off a mark, pull a heist."

"Easy with that," I said. I looked around at the

tables. People were talking among themselves, the bouzouki band was going, and only one couple was dancing. Then I saw Abe going past the tables, just able to get his big belly by them.

Abe, a tall guy, round-shouldered and sloppy fat, had a face on him that looked like it had been squeezed together, his eyes popping, lips so fat that when he talked it was a little spitty. He was a mover of paper scores, stocks and bonds, and Treasury E bonds. With the fugazy, phony papers, he could move anything.

I pulled out a chair for him. He sat, bringing himself closer to me. Before he could say anything, I told him, "Got nothing for you."

"Got to score someplace. I'm tapped out," he said.

"Who isn't? You know how it's been. Haven't seen good paper in months."

"Got to get something soon."

"We all do."

"Well, if you land something, you know where to reach me."

"Sure, Abe. First thing," I said.

He moved off to another table and sat with some people. I tried calling my wife. I'd tried an hour before and it was busy. I got another busy. When I tried again, it finally rang. I asked, "What's happening over there?"

Kitty said she could hardly hear me with all the noise.

"Who were you talking to?"

"Dottie."

"For over an hour?"

"Over two hours."

"What're you, her priest, her psychiatrist?"

That was my wife, all right. Dottie, Bobby Boriello's wife, would talk and talk for hours, mostly griping about her old man, and my old lady would just listen. She was some good listener. She'd listen to anybody's troubles. I could never understand why. Dottie and Kitty had nothing in common. Dottie was always bitching, while the old lady would never bitch about anything, and Dottie was ten years younger than my wife.

Kitty's birthday was coming up in August, and I said maybe I'd take her to dinner or something, but we couldn't just go by ourselves. Maybe I'd bring Joey and a couple of guys and their wives. She didn't say anything right off. I put another dime in the phone. Then she said she'd rather we went alone, and I said if we could we would. We weren't like other people. She said that was just the damned trouble. I told her it was better if a lot of the guys came along, and anyway it was a chance for everyone to unwind.

I saw Louie the Syrian and some of the guys outside the phone booth, talking to Bobby Darrow. I told my old lady I'd talk about it later, about finding a nice place to go for her birthday.

I asked Louie to think of something nice to get the old lady for her birthday. He shrugged and said just about anything, that the important thing was just remembering. Louie the Syrian, who had eleven kids, really loved his family. But he was separated from his wife, so I guess he wasn't the guy to ask.

He thanked me and said his brother-in-law Sammy wanted to thank me for breaking up the fight over at his place, that it would have brought heat if Bobby Boriello had shot Little Freddy. Well, they didn't have to worry about that, I told him. Joey had chased the kid. Louie felt that was a shame, that Little Freddy would be all right if he was a little more sensible. I said maybe he was the one that was sensible.

The night of my wife's birthday, we ended up as ten couples going over to the Chateau Madrid for dinner, then over to Port Said for the belly dancer. We'd taken ringside tables. One of our crew would stay at the bar, making sure who was coming in, and then another would go to the bar, and the first would come back.

When the show started, the bouzouki band accompanied the belly dancer. Then she went over backward, her head touching the floor, a Greek standing over her, throwing dollar bills on her belly. Joey liked that, all right.

Afterward she went to every table and stood swaying, her arms outstretched, slowly clicking those brass cymbals on her fingers. Money had been tucked along her waist. By the time she reached our tables she seemed to have more green than gold sequins, with all the folded money along her shoulder straps and bra and all around her waist. Bobby Darrow took a five, ran it along her belly, then tucked it in the center at her waist, and you just knew he wanted to give her a pat right below. That was when she backed off, really slamming those cymbals, ringing in his face.

We were having a time. I started to get stoned. I felt like I was letting go. I kept asking my wife, "Having a good time?" and she kept saying she was. Now she was telling me to take it easy, while I said, "Why take it easy? We never have to take it easy."

I was letting go, all right, and when the dancing started, it was a syrto. Who but a Greek can dance the syrto? The dancers, in a long line, bobbed each other's hands in time to the bouzouki band while I led them, holding the end of the handkerchief, held by my wife. I was really dancing, bringing my knees up high, slapping the heel of my shoe, then going under the handkerchief, hissing through my teeth, then going "Oppa!" each time I did.

They they played the theme music from *Zorba the Greek*. I did a mean syrtaki, clicking my fingers over my head, going faster, still staying with it, not as drunk as I thought. Greeks were throwing money on the floor, going "Oppa! Oppa!", clapping their hands, stamping their feet in time.

When I stopped, my head kept spinning. They were all standing, applauding, Joey leading them after he'd said, "And if anybody doesn't like my Greek and doesn't applaud"—with that smiling way of his, eyeing every table—"I'm going to burn the place down."

Then the owner sent over several bottles of wine, while a couple of friends of mine, two Greeks, came over to talk to my wife. Joey leaned over, saying, "Listen, don't introduce me to any assholes. This is your town, these are your people. Just make sure—"

"Hey, Joey, these are two good guys. Did I ever introduce you to any assholes? So what are you talking about?"

He grinned. "You cocky Greek. It's a good thing I really like you. It's a good thing."

One of the Greeks whispered to me, saying the pistols I kept stashed in his taverna, he'd get them, and when we were ready to leave they'd watch the door. I answered him in Greek that he was being foolish, that he didn't know about such things.

I told Joey how they were willing to extend themselves.

"You're right, Greek. These are good guys. You know how to pick them. You usually pick good guys."

"Good people, my people," I said, "but very foolish sometimes."

1972

twelve

The writer our crew would have loved giving a beating to was Jimmy Breslin, who wrote *The Gang That Couldn't Shoot Straight*. We loved a lot of parts in that, like when we came off falling all over ourselves, spaghetti getting thrown in our faces, and from thirty feet, none of us could hit the side of a country billboard. Or that funny part about Junior Persico—some guy who was supposed to be Junior—when he blew up after we piped his car, only there was just smoke and noise, and Junior, it seemed, just got out brushing himself off. The whole thing was funny. The Profaci war was just a bunch of laughs. Well, Breslin should have spent one night with us, found out what it would feel like if some Profaci clipped him in the ass. Even with a small Baretta, he wouldn't be fucking laughing.

When they made the flick, they even had the balls to film it around President Street. They weren't about to tell us what or who it was all about. There wasn't anything real about it—with its made-up, red-faced actors in big gray fedoras, wearing suits with pinstripes that looked like they'd been drawn with chalk—except for a dwarf that looked a little like Armando. We'd see them around with their trucks, and wires all over the place, actors sitting around in canvas chairs, and we'd ask what kind of movie they were making, and they'd say a comedy. They hated like hell to tell us anything.

The movie was going to premiere on Broadway. We thought of hiring two big black limousines, dressing up in tuxedoes with big white gardenias in our lapels, smoking big cigars, and then crowning all that with the dwarf, Armando, since he was supposed to be in the flick too. We'd have him in a tux, a big comic cigar, almost as big as him, touting a kid's plastic sub-Thompson, and then going to the show. Well, we only joked about it.

One night, with Papa Gallo up front, we headed over to Court Street. I had one eye on the rear-view mirror, keeping a space between us and the car in front, giving myself enough room in case shooters jumped out, staying in the left lane so nobody could make us so easy and I could swing around into the oncoming lane if I had to. We were talking about the goddamned flick of Breslin's when I almost went into this red sports car that cut in front of me. Bobby Darrow, in the back, already had the girlfriend leveled over the seat. Papa Gallo jolted upright.

It was only some kid with whiskers. His car was angled in, almost broadside, and he was yelling, "You flaky or something? Watch where the fuck you're driving!"

Joey rolled down the back window. "All right, darling. Anything else you want?"

The kid, driving off, muttered something, giving us the middle finger.

Joey let loose in Italian, saying up his hairy asshole and fuck his sister in hers. Then he laid a hand on my shoulder. "Greek, will you please watch where you're going? That guy looked like he'd destroy us."

Bobby snickered. Papa Gallo was sitting rigid in the seat, as though he was still looking back at the barrel, even though Bobby had put it away.

After I found a place to park, I checked out

front and had Bobby stash the pistol. Then we all went
into the Queen Restaurant. People from the DA's office
came there to eat. We ate there often. We were used
to being stared at.

We'd taken our table at the rear left when I saw
this guy and this tall job, a big face on her, come in.
Joey held up his hand, and the guy, raising his chin,
came over smiling. The broad was damned uneasy.

Bobby whispered, "Who the fuck are them people?"

"Wait till you hear this," I said.

At the table they shook hands. The tall broad
gave a little nod, trying to smile. Joey was standing,
introducing us all around. We didn't do much of anything. They were Marta and Jerry Orbach, the woman
a little high-sounding. I didn't like meeting people like
that. Bobby leaned over again, his eyes on the table.
"So who are they?" Then giving me his ear.

I held up my hand to wait.

Seated at the table, the broad still had that look
about her. "Relax," Joey told her. "You've got nothing
to worry about here."

She looked around at all the tables as though she
expected shooters. "Seems a lot of people know you.
Bit of a celebrity."

The waiter stood at the table. Joey suggested the
scungilli, the calamari, the spaghetti with clam sauce,
and the wine. After the waiter had the order, Jerry
Orbach said, "Well, to be perfectly frank, Mr. Gallo—"

"Joey."

"—we couldn't resist your invitation."

"I'm glad."

"We were very curious."

"Extremely," said this Marta Orbach.

She was some big woman. Bobby Darrow was beginning to stare at them. I kicked his shoe under the
table.

After we opened the wine and began to eat, Joey
said to Jerry Orbach, "So, you're Kid Sally Palumbo."

He was talking about the part Orbach played in
The Gang That Couldn't Shoot Straight. In it Joey—if
anybody could believe it—was supposed to be Kid

Sally Palumbo. It was bad enough that "Palumbo" sounded like "Colombo." He'd been more than just angry with that flick, but he was also curious when he invited the Orbachs to dinner. He'd told me there was a long pause when he did.

Joey, with that smile, asked this Jerry, "Whatever made you play such an asshole—excuse me, Marta —a part like that?"

"Well, the part came along, bit low on funds, and the bread was good."

"Yeah?" That was an answer he liked. "But you're the actor. I'm the real guy."

Soon the Orbachs began calling him by his first name. I kept my eye on the front and kitchen doors. To them I must have looked asleep. I caught Marta smiling over. I looked at the front door again.

"Tell me, Joey," said Jerry. "Is it true that you kept a lion in your cellar?"

"Yeah, at Armando's, our dwarf. He's our friend."

"A lion, a full-grown lion?"

"About three-fourths."

"Male?"

"Guys that didn't pay the vig, the poor payers, were sent down to the lion. It got everybody to pay up. Now you don't believe that story, do you?"

"Sounds too incredible."

"We had the lion, only we had to get rid of it."

"But you really had a lion?"

"Sure. Everybody knew it."

Marta gave a little laugh. She seemed to have a nice way about her. Joey began rapping heavy when she told him she was a writer of sorts, and he asked what she thought of Hemingway, then Sartre and Camus. I saw her fork go down. Bobby's shoe touched mine and he asked if the last thing was an aftershave.

Marta was looking at Joey differently. You naturally did when he started talking that way. Papa Gallo said, "One smart boy I got."

"Surprising," said Marta.

I wasn't listening or understanding it that well. Joey asked her who was the better writer and the better man, Sartre or this Camus. Then he wondered if the works of Hemingway and this Camus weren't deceptions when they both ultimately betrayed themselves by committing suicide. Marta said this Camus was killed in a car accident. Joey told her it was intentional suicide.

That was the way they were rapping, with Bobby Darrow rolling his eyes to the ceiling. Then Marta asked Joey if he ever considered doing his memoirs.

"My *what?*"

"Your memoirs."

"Is there any money in it?"

She told him there'd be a lot in something like that. I began to listen. She knew publishers who would be ecstatic with the idea. Then I wasn't listening. I was listening to the part about the money.

She caught me looking at her as she reached for the bread. She almost stopped. Then she pulled off a slice and only picked at it, saying it was fattening, guessed it was her Italian heritage to be a big woman. She gave me another look, then at the breadbasket. She might have sensed something. I don't think she ever knew.

We'd only brought in one pistol, mine, and I had the girlfriend under the napkin in the breadbasket so the law wouldn't find it on me, and so I could get the thirty-eight out fast if Colombo people came in.

During those winter months Joey was in the papers a lot, far more than he ever had been. But he was always in the papers, and as far back as the Profaci war the Gallo wine people must have changed their labels to Ernest and Julio Gallo so that no one would think their wine was connected to Joey Gallo. It was a common enough name, and a few who had it either hid from it or were embarrassed, but most claimed to be related, Joey suddenly had an awful lot of relatives, and new friends.

It was the Orbachs who started him hobnobbing with a lot of big people, like Ben Gazzara, Peter Falk, and actress Joan Hackett, who loved Joey calling her

a broad. Then there was some author named Bruce
Jay Friedman, a playwright named Neil Simon, a pub-
lisher by the name of Tom Guinzburg, comedian David
Steinberg, and all sorts of such people. We were going
to classy dinners and parties, and you weren't in if
Joey wasn't coming to yours.

Marta Orbach had set a standard of particulars (I
think that was what she called it) on how her friends
should conduct themselves with him, and she wouldn't
invite just anyone. If it wasn't bouncing at some night-
clubs or dinner parties at Ben Gazzara's or Tom Guinzburg's, it was dropping in on Marta at all hours, or
having Sunday dinners with her family. Once Joey
showed up in his peaked cap and leather jacket. From
then on Marta was in jeans and an old sweater and
was always trying to give him an old-fashioned Italian
Sunday dinner. She didn't think he'd particularly go
for servants waiting on him with Baccarat crystal.

At those parties Joey would be in the middle of
everything, rapping about everything there was—life,
politics, books, plays, or some fucking artist long dead.
He'd have all kinds of people around him, and you'd
find yourself giving him a double take and a third. That
was Joey too. There was a lot to him. Nobody could
be a bad guy, a wiseguy, twenty-four hours a day, and
there he'd be: smooth, articulate, a charming bastard.
Still, I could never get over it, and I suppose I knew
him as well as anyone.

I could never understand what kind of charge
anyone got out of it. Maybe they liked being around a
guy who was up for the shot, or maybe they had the
stupid idea that they were immune from it and, like
most people, thought that wiseguys only kill wiseguys.

Maybe he came off like some kind of freak to
them. They could never get over how brilliant and
charming he was, some shit like that, something that
Marta started. But he never overheard the crap of
how small he was, how hard it was to imagine him a
gangster murdering anyone, or how he was like Lucifer
holding court.

It was at one of those parties that a limp blonde

came over and asked me, "Are you really an associate of Joey's?" I looked at her and said nothing, while her boyfriend took her by the arm, pulling her away. Then over by the grand piano, while somebody was playing some cornball, she came alongside. I said, "Hey."

"Hmmm?"

"Want to fuck?"

"Of course," she said. Then she pointed her cocktail at her boyfriend. "But I'm with him."

That's about what Joey would have asked if anybody got to him. Then he'd go over to a corner and sit by himself. Marta got it around that he was shy, and something about him having sad, sad eyes.

Joey called her Big Mama or the Tall Job, and she would try to be very gracious and make you feel comfortable. But I never felt very comfortable. I was on a different planet.

Marta was also the one who started Joey on the whole dumb idea of writing his memoirs, saying she would write them. It made wiseguys nervous. Ubatz, the crazy one, they said, was ubatz for sure. Walsh, the FBI guy on the block, said he thought it would make interesting reading. Very interesting.

The first time Joey talked about it, we were over at his flat. He asked me what I thought of the idea.

"Hey, Joey," I said.

"What's this, 'Hey, Joey?' "

"This broad, Marta, she's going to write it?"

"Yeah."

"And she knows mob guys, how they do things and how they think? What makes her so special? She's Italian. Ungots, she knows. Writing about you is like writing about the atom bomb without knowing anything about it. Are you fucking serious?"

"Sure I'm serious. I want to know what you think."

"You really want to know? All right. Have you ever known me to lie to you, hold back on anything? And you want to know what I think, right? You're out of your fucking tree, that's what I think. What're you going to write about? The old man? Genovese? Profaci?"

"I'm sticking just to Joey Gallo."

"Oh, just Joey Gallo? Uh-huh. All right. Let's start with a good part of the story. Outside the barbershop." I took my pinky. "Joe Jelly's at the wheel." Then my fourth finger. "Here's your brother Larry." Then my middle. "And here's you," corkscrewing it. "Right up your ass they'll put it when you write that."

I took my forefinger. "Now it's been arranged for the bodyguard to take the walk. He goes for the convenient cup of coffee. You look around. No law, or you got them laying off, arranged so they don't come up so fast. Now you see your opportunity. You and your brother, set to go in, pull up the scarfs covering your faces, and out come the pistols. Already you know he's in the fourth barber chair, hot towel or no hot towel. And who told you he's in the fourth chair? The bodyguard. You come in fast. Boom, boom, boom. You go out fast. A good piece of work. And *who* did you just clip?" I took my thumb, waving it at him. "Anastasia. *This* is what you're going to write about?"

"Hey, I'm not that crazy, Greek."

"Oh, no? Then that's good. But what are you going to write about? What *can* you write? What can you even say?"

"Nothing."

"How can you write about nothing?"

"Easy. People do it all the time," he said.

The Viking Press was going to come up with a lot of bread for Joey's book. They loved the idea. Well, we loved it too. Joey dragged me around to some publishing attorney. Afterward I only talked to him when I had to and didn't really say anything until we got back to his flat. He asked what was biting me, and I said nothing was biting me, just those guys he talked about, like that Kafka guy, Céline, and the aftershave, Camus. Guys like that had nothing to worry about, that is, big dons like the old man, Carlo Gambino.

The same afternoon, he had us take him over to
Viking Press. We stayed out in the hall. I read some
magazine, while Bobby Darrow eyed the broad at the
desk, who wasn't much. Then they came out laughing.
Marta stayed back, talking to some guy. Joey put his
arm around my shoulders. "Greek, you sweet sonofabitch. I feel good."

"You feel good."

"You know, there's something suicidal about publishers, paying a lot of greens for the big nothing."

"Hope it's the big nothing. Let's get out of here."

Marta came over just then. He put his arm around
her too. "What do you think of my Greek here?"

"Quiet, charming in an ominous way."

I had them step to the side of the elevator. You
never knew who was coming out. "Sorry," I said, "just
doing my job."

A couple of days later Stanley the Jew called.
"Greek?"

"Yeah."

"We're ready. Got something good."

"Watch it. Listen, I'll be down around three. You
know where."

Bobby Darrow and I had to go over to pick up
Joey. I told him we had a giveup and we'd be by later
or call some of the guys for him. He said he was coming along. "There's money?" he said. "I'm going."

"Joey, let's not have another Teddy Moss over
here," I told him. He never would have been nailed for
extortion if he had listened to his brother Larry, who
had told him to send some of the guys to go on Moss.
A boss never went on a piece of work, but Joey was
unorthodox. "You don't want to get yourself nailed
again," I said.

"Fuck it," he said. "I'm going."

Over at this ginmill Stanley the Jew was by the
bar, wearing a dingy peaked cap with union buttons. He
needed a shave. He looked at Joey, who had the same
cap and jacket, only neater, and headed for the back.
I told Joey, "Stay at the bar with Bobby. Do me a
favor."

"The guy doesn't know me."

"It's bad enough he knows *me*. And he'll remember that mole."

"So he'll remember it."

"Will you listen to me? Stay here. I have to do the talking anyway."

"All right," he said.

Stanley was at the back table, acting as though he wasn't watching us. A trucker, gypsy mostly, but a wheeler-dealer, he worked the giveup. You know, pretending to be hijacked. He was standup, could take questioning, and the lie detector. I'd worked him a couple of times.

With his arms folded on the table, he managed to keep looking away from Joey and Bobby Darrow at the bar when I asked, "You got the giveup?"

"No, a friend of mine."

"Who's the friend?"

"Pat. We've partnered before. He's all right."

"Hey, we're only doing business with you. I don't want to see your partner, and I don't want him to see us."

"Who's going to ride him off?"

"We'll get somebody. So what's the load?"

"Good. Olive oil and tomatoes."

"That's a good load. Very good."

"A full rig, fourteen high, forty-foot bed. It'll bring in plenty. You got the drop and the buy?"

"Give us a couple of hours. We'll have both. Your friend gets nervous around a pistol?"

"You don't have to heist it. Just pick him up and I'll bring her in."

"Stanley, he'll remember the pistol when he takes the lie detector," I told him. "Stay here. We'll let you know where and what. Don't make any calls and watch for law."

When we left, Joey asked, "Who've you got to pick up his partner?"

"Crazy Ang, a Greek. He won't rat us out."

Over on Utica Avenue we went into another gin-mill and saw the buy, Big Tony. I told him about the load. Big Tony, smoking a cigar, was by the cash register counting money, not looking at us. "My brother's garage in Williamsburg. Make the drop. What time you figure?"

"When it's dark," I said. " 'Round seven. We'll be there."

"Bring the money," said Joey.

That night Joey and I tailed the rig over to the garage in Williamsburg. I said to Joey, "Get off that fucking book. You *can't* write it. You know why. You'll get some bad shit out of it, worse than Colombo."

"Greek, you worry too much. I told you. I'm giving them the big nothing. Just about Attica and Auburn, about the yard, the black wall, the PR wall, and the white wall, and make it all into a black comedy. The nine and a half I did in the slams, that's all. Just some Jimmy Breslin bullshit. Don't *ever* think I'm giving them anything else."

"They'll want more."

"Don't worry. No Family business."

"Well, I wouldn't want you to write about this," I said.

I'd already smashed the front speedometer of the rig with the jimmy, and the meter on the rear wheels, so the law could never know by the mileage where the drop was once we dumped the truck.

When we got to the garage, Stanley was backing her in beautifully until the roof slammed into the entrance way. It was too high to clear. Traffic had stopped. We kept an eye out for sector cars while Stanley let some of the air out of the tires. She was loaded. Empty she would have been almost a foot too high. Then Stanley backed her in, with nothing to spare. I had Joey wait in the car with Bobby.

Big Tony and four kids were standing around, waiting to unload. With the jimmy, I pulled down the lock till it snapped. The rig was loaded, mostly olive oil.

The kids had the first row out and were working the second. Then they had both. One of the kids came out. "Better look see."

"Whatsamatter?" I asked.

"Just look."

I got up on the tailgate. Then I saw what it was.
I pulled out one carton, then the carton behind that,
trying to get to the third.

"What the fuck is it?" asked Big Tony.

I came off the tailgate, disgusted. "Matches," I
said. "Nothing but fucking matches."

We had the rig in Jersey, over on a lot. You
could see gas refineries. It was flat country. Fires were
burning from tall stacks, lighting everything a dirty
yellow. Well, there was going to be another fire.

Ripping down a bedsheet, I twisted it like a wick,
setting it under the match crates, letting it hang off
the tailgate. Then Bobby Darrow slopped gas along
the crates, then into the back of the rig, throwing in
can and all. Gas had gotten on his pants and shoes. He
was sopping with it. I called him a meatball, and had
him head for the car before he went up with it.

He was clear. I lit the tail and ran.

I had the wheel, barreling the Caddy, when it
blew, lighting the sky with one hell of a thump, pieces
flying, the whole trailer just jerking up in the air, down
onto the cab, then over on its side. Those matches went
up like a bomb.

Bobby looked back at the fire. You could still see
it a long way off.

When we got back to Dolly's, Joey asked about
Stanley, then said, "Didn't that asshole partner of his
check the manifest? I don't understand it."

"What're you asking me for?" I said. "I'm not
working on eight pistons with you writing your book."

Stanley the Jew felt bad about what had gone
down with the giveup. I felt bad. He said maybe, just
maybe, he could work up a mark who was into buying
North Carolina smokes by truckloads, paying ninety
cents to a buck a carton. It could bring twenty-five to
thirty thou for a load. I told him, good, work him, and
when he was ready we'd rent a rig and use Big Tony's
drop in Williamsburg. Stanley said to make sure it was
only twelve high, didn't want the same problem we
had before. I didn't have to tell him that the first row
would be cigarettes, and behind that empty cases.

When he'd set up the mark, he called me at Dolly's. I told him in an hour. We took off the two-hundred-dollar suits (which were swag anyway) and the gold watches and diamond pinky rings, dressed up in suits that looked like fifty dollars and dark ties and plain fedoras. This time Bobby Darrow and I were bringing Joey Balzano: tall, potbellied, an around guy who really looked like law.

On the way over to the ginmill we rehearsed it. Once the rig pulled into the front of the garage, we'd wait three, maybe two minutes before coming in from the side. Stanley would play the mark. He'd tell him he wanted to get the greens, didn't care what the guy did with the rig after that. He'd play it nervous, and that was important, saying he could do ten federal at least for what he was doing and just wanted to get the hell out of here, and maybe saying something like he wouldn't be doing what he was doing if he wasn't into the shylocks.

Then two, three minutes, and maybe just when he's gotten the rig opened, we would come in from the side, yelling we're the law and flashing pistols and shields. A jittery bird to begin with, Stanley would start running along the loading platform like a fucking bastard, trying to make it out the door. Only Balzano pegs two shots in the air, yelling the next one goes up his ass, and Stanley hits the floor. He's just scared shit, the arms go up, and he's screaming, "See? They're up! They're up!" Then he gets diarrhea of the mouth, like Joe Valachi.

He's yelling that the mark was buying the whole load, a hijacked load. He's cooperating and he yells where the greens are, which, naturally, we confiscate as evidence. The mark now wants his out, naturally. Balzano is bad law, while Darrow and I are nice reasonable cops, trying to keep Balzano from killing him. When the mark talks deal, Balzano goes into a bribery bit. Besides we need the collar. A collar like this will make us first grade. Balzano will sell his fucking mother to make first grade. We're acquainted with the type, as I'm sure the mark is. Then the mark tries harder, and naturally we—especially Balzano—finally give into temptation, the greens, and we'd work it from there. I asked them if they got all that.

"Yeah, yeah," said Bobby Darrow. "Jesus Christ, yeah."

At the ginmill Stanley the Jew headed for the back when he saw us come in. He sat down at the table, all the while eyeing Joey Balzano. It was the first time he'd seen him.

"What're you staring at?" Balzano asked him.

"Nothing."

"What're you thinking, Stanley?" I asked.

"Him. He's law."

"That's right, Stanley," I said. "The badass, motherfucking law. A *real* badass."

Joey Balzano smiled.

"Stanley," I said, "he's not going to be smiling."

"Shit," said Stanley, "I would have fucked a syphed-up cunt just to get outta here."

"That's the idea, Stanley."

"He looks so much like law," said Bobby Darrow, "he never can get a hooker to blow him."

"You would think of that," I said. "Come on, Stanley. Let's move on the mark."

"Can I have a drink first?" Stanley asked. "I think I need one."

thirteen

After we'd taken off the mark, we went over to Joey's apartment. He wasn't around. I didn't have to ask his wife where he was. Jeffie was edgy, yelling at her daughter, who was crying. She buttoned the kid's coat, really pulling on the buttons, then dragged her to the door. When she was aware of us, Jeffie said, "Sorry, Pete," trying to get herself together. "Guess you'll wait."

"Yeah," I said, feeling awkward.

"Like I'm waiting. Why don't you just call upstairs to his hillbilly whore?"

She shoved the kid out the door, then slammed it hard.

When Joey had first gone to the can, Jeffie was seeing him as often as she could, and he'd asked her if she was going to be stupid and wait around for ten years. Every time she came, he'd get rougher with her, until he finally asked her why she was coming around bothering him, just so he'd see what she had, when he couldn't do anything, and he'd go on about getting herself a divorce, finding some asshole, and not bothering him anymore, that he didn't even want to see her.

Well, she'd come down to President Street crying, telling his brother Larry about it. It hadn't been easy on her and that last time had been too much. Larry had told her that his crazy brother really loved her, but he really didn't want to hurt her, waiting all those years for him, that it had been rough on her, but it must have been a lot rougher for him to chase her away.

For years we didn't see her after that. We heard later about the divorce and that she'd married some English guy with money. That must have been some marriage. It lasted as long as Joey was in the slams. When she heard he was coming out, she divorced the Englishman.

When she told Joey she had gotten rid of her husband, he said, "Yeah?" Then, "Why?" And when she told him straight out that she still loved him, he said, "Kook." Later he told me that there was something special about her, standing up all that time and waiting. Then, as though all that embarrassed him, he said, "Yeah, but there must be something wrong with that stupid broad."

At first they moved in with Mama Gallo, but Joey didn't get along too well with his mother. So Jeffie found them a place in Manhattan on West Fourteenth Street, just off Fifth. It was really a nice apartment, and it was near Greenwich Village. Joey had always liked the Village, and Jeffie dressed like she was Village. Dark, but green eyed, she was awfully pretty, with nice curves to her.

Joey had his Uncle Joe Iovine make the arrangements, and they were remarried in a civil ceremony. For about a month after they moved into the new apartment, he seemed almost domesticated and very happy and only liked being with Jeffie and his daughter. Then, when everything seemed to be going right, he called me one day and said he'd chased Jeffie. When I asked what had happened, he said he didn't want to talk about it and told me to come over with Darrow.

In his living room he was lying on the sofa, his feet up on the bolster, a wine glass on his chest. He didn't say anything for a long time. Then he sat up, his head jerking to one side everytime he slammed the heel of his palm on his knee. "That dirty! Miserable! No good! Fucking *cunt!* I'm a rotten bastard, and she comes back loving it. I'm nice, and she comes back a no-good rotten bitch. Hey, she's got my balls twisted. I had to get her the fuck out of here, or I'd have thrown her out of the window. Told her to stay away for a week, and not to call, not to do anything for a week. Hey, she's in my hair every fucking minute. She don't let up."

"I know," I said. I liked Jeffie, I really did, but she was so standup, she had to say what she had to, and she'd say it to anybody, even Joey.

Joey, then, was only a couple of months out of the slams, and I'd told him what he really needed was a lot of exercise, that he must have had nearly ten years of starch in him, unless he'd worked Mary Fist or had his boy ass in the slams. "Get off that boy-ass shit," he told me. Then he said, "I see you're exercising. I never know where to call you, your wife's or your gum-mare's."

Well, I told him if he wanted to catch up with me, he had to start now. Besides he'd feel better.

I called this Desmond. I told him I wanted three especially nice. He said he had two nice white chicks, and asked if I was prejudiced.

"Talking to you, aren't I?" I said. "Like all that chocolate and vanilla. Mix it all up."

"Man, you *are* bad," he said. Then he told me where.

Over on the corner of Thirty-fourth Street and Third, Desmond, in a gray-white furry fedora and all in silky black with a peace cross at his throat, the horn, and a lot of other stuff, came over to my cab, looking over his shoulder. The three were standing under an awning, showing a lot of leg. The black broad was the only one wearing boots, white boots, and had lashes an inch long.

Desmond stood under the awning with his hands in his pockets as we drove off. One blonde kept working her lips into a compact mirror. The black broad put her arm around me. Her perfume was cheap crap. I told her I wasn't the john. The john was a friend of mine who owned a furniture store and needed some diversion.

"Baby," she said, "we're all going with one stud, this here Mr. Furniture Man? He ain't no freak now?"

"No, but you got to party."

"She-it. Party us three? Baby, that's expensive."

I told her Desmond had set the price for partying. Besides they'd have food and drink, a nice pad, and they wouldn't have to kick in to Desmond.

"Yeah? And who is this that Desmond is doing *this* for?"

"Mr. Furniture Man," I said.

When the taxi pulled up, Joey was at his apartment window, grinning and waving, then threw the sofa's bolster, hitting the roof of the taxi. The black broad said, "Baby, now I thought you done tol' me that this here Mr. Furniture Man ain't no freak."

"Baby, he's just happy."

"She-it," she said.

Bobby Darrow and I stayed out in the living room. You could hear them at first inside the bedroom. Then you heard nothing. Bobby was going a little crazy, but I said, "Well, at least it's getting Jeffie off his mind."

Most of the time they got on pretty well, but at the New Year's Eve party at Dolly's, Jeffie started giving mouth. He told her at least three times to shut up. She wasn't shutting up for him or anybody. He grabbed her, taking her inside the other room, and started belting the hell out of her. I got between them before he killed her. She still wouldn't shut up and was letting loose about Sina, yelling that hillbilly, that whore, the dentist who'd paid her rent, to want that whore over her, to do something like that to her. And Joey was still trying to get at her, and I was saying, "Joey, please. Please, Joey. She's hurt." And he was yelling to get her the fuck out of his sight before he really did a number on her.

Well, I knew about Sina, all right. She was the dentist's receptionist.

It wasn't long after he moved into his new apartment that he started visiting the dentist in the same building, mainly because he'd said his teeth had saved his life in the slams. I suppose he was talking about the time he bit a guy's ear off. So he was seeing the dentist to have his teeth capped. It was going to cost him something like five thousand dollars. He was taking good care of them, all right, but that wasn't all he was taking care of.

At her desk, you couldn't help noticing Sina: dark-haired, pretty, soft, with lovely curves to her, and an awfully nice way of speaking. She didn't seem to belong there. Joey liked her more and more, then began seeing her.

But she had the penthouse in his building. I found out later that it went for five hundred a month, while Joey was paying something like three hundred for his. So once, when Sina was out of the room, I asked what came naturally. How could this broad afford the penthouse? Joey explained that it was the dentist, only he couldn't be coming around anymore. Then he'd say nice things about her, yet end it typically by saying, "But she's a fucking hillbilly from Ohio."

He started to go heavy on her. I could understand it. You didn't feel around Sina as you would with the Orbachs, although after a while I started to get used to Marta and her crowd, and even liked some of them. Sina was something else altogether. You liked her right off. But you knew that Jeffie would never stand for it.

I told him Jeffie wasn't about to be the wife downstairs with a gummare upstairs. That would be too much for her to take, and it was. She came after Sina.

I'd heard about it over at Greek Town when I made my rounds, collecting some vig money. Outside an Egyptian restaurant, one of my people said Joey was up there. I asked, "What Joey?"

"Your boss. What other Joey is there?"

Upstairs, at the far corner near the bandstand,

Joey sat at a table with his usual leather jacket and peaked cap. He was crooking his neck around one of those synthetic palm trees when he made me. Pulling out a chair, he said, "She told you, didn't she? Jeffie told you I was here."

"Some Greek told me. Good thing he's one of my people and he didn't tell anybody else."

When I sat alongside, he twisted my cheek, patting me on the shoulder. "Christ, I'm stoned. I'm fucking stoned. Wanted to get my head straight. I got it screwed up straight. That fucking broad. Don't know what I'm going to do with her. Hey, Greek, know I chased her when I was in the slams?"

"Yeah, I know."

"Lousy things I said to her. Knew she was making it with some guy. Guess I always knew. Well, she's human. She's got to get the itch. And what can I do when I know I've got at least ten big ones to do? Can't ship it to her in an envelope. So I chased her. Then seeing her again, I thought it would work out. Hey, fuck that bullshit. Let's go someplace and eat."

"Why anyplace else? Eat right here. We'll have some good feta cheese, calamata olives, stuffed grape leaves with a little lemon. You'll like that. Make a Greek out of you."

"Sounds good, not being a Greek."

Afterward he said, "Know what Jeffie did? She came up to Sina's apartment. I gave her some beating, so I'm here getting stoned. Hey, I don't want to hurt her, and I know I really will if she keeps on, but she won't let up. Who needs this bullshit? Hey, you got your gummare and Kitty doesn't say anything."

"She doesn't say it. But she doesn't like it."

"A lot for a woman to take. Who'd take that from a woman? Not fair. So the only fair thing to do is chase the bitch," he said.

He didn't chase her right off. It was on again, off again. Sometimes I felt he was in love with both Jeffie and Sina, but he treated both of them different-ly. With Jeffie he would brawl. With Sina he was easy, but all he had to do was say one lousy thing, and not too lousy at that, and she'd be crying. I think he needed them both.

He loved Sina's daughter, Lisa, and he went all out, doing all he could for her. She was a very mature child, very talented, into TV commercials, and was just starting in some stage play. Over at Sardi's we were waiting for the reviews to come in, when Joey asked if Sinatra was in town.

"How would I know if Sinatra's in town?" I said. "What am I, a singer?"

"Come on, Greek. He always goes to Jilly's when he comes to town."

"Joey, this is embarrassing, sitting with all these theatrical people. I mean, not embarrassing sitting here, but acting like them, waiting for reviews. What're we in now, show business?"

"But don't you think Sinatra can help the kid?"

"Yeah, him and all the wiseguys."

Whenever Frank Sinatra was in town, he'd usually stop at Jilly's on the West Side, a hangout for all too many wiseguys. All we had to do was go there, and somebody could drop a dime on us, call Eighty-sixth Street, and we'd be looking at Colombo shooters. He knew that as well as I did. He wanted to go anyway.

Not less than three of us were going to Jilly's. When we came in Jilly, with his yellow glasses, wasn't anywhere around. Neither was Sinatra at his usual table, but there were plenty of wiseguys. It was like a convention. Afterward Joey laid a fifty on the doorman, taking him by the lapels, pulling him close. The doorman was to say nothing to nobody, but when Sinatra was in town, he was to call Louie the Syrian. That was a fifty thrown out the window. That doorman would never call.

When we left him off by his apartment door that night, he said to me, "Greek, stay close, be cool, and I'll see you tomorrow."

fourteen

We were coming back one night from one of those parties that Marta usually arranged. I was getting a little more than annoyed with all that crap, and I asked Joey, "Will you tell me something? What in the fuck are we doing with those people?"

He wouldn't answer me. When I got him back to his apartment, I asked him again. He said we were the connection.

"What connection?"

"Believe me, Greek, these people are no different from anybody else. They have a problem, and they don't know what to do. Say it's serious. They go to the lawyer, or they go to the law. What do they get? They get jerked around. What does the lawyer do? Nothing. What does the law do? Same thing. Or say a guy's got a problem with his old lady. She's fucking around. It's eating him up when there's nothing he can do about it, except maybe punch the other guy in the mouth, which can get him six months in the workhouse —that is, if the guy fucking with his wife has political connections. Or say he needs fast greens, but he's over-extended, and the bank gives him ungots, and even talks about taking his business if he doesn't come up with the greens he owes, and they've been robbing him right along with the big interest.

"Now, though, he's got us. Now he knows where to go. The bank won't give him, so we do, and instead of the bank robbing him, we're robbing him. That guy that's fucking with his old lady? For a good price, we bust the guy's arms. And suppose he wants us to do a final on the guy. Now he knows he can talk to us about a thing like that. So we negotiate and we take the guy off. Or say the guy's got a big insurance policy and nothing else, and he wants to make sure his family is taken care of. He can't do it himself. There's a suicide clause. So we do it for him. Anything, Greek, anything he couldn't do before, now he can with us."

"That's why?"

"Well, partly."

"Know what? Next time you go to one of those parties, know what you do? You put on your dark pin-stripe suit, a dark shirt and white tie, and don't forget your fucking dark glasses."

When they called him in front of the McClellan Committee in D.C. years back, that's exactly what he wore. He'd told his brother Larry, "They want to see a gangster? That's how I'm going—looking like one."

He wasn't always happy with Marta Orbach, although he liked her most of the time. Just as he could turn on you in one second, he'd say she was acting the way a man should act. Once when she was pushing him too hard on that book, he came into Dolly's, saying, "That big job acts likes she's married to me, like she wants to put my two feet in one shoe. Know what she needs? A good hump. Greek, go throw her a hump." When I said, "No way," he told Bobby Darrow, who'd screw anything, but he said, "Not me either."

I really didn't know what was going on with that book, and the less I knew the better, but Joey started talking about canning her, getting another writer who understood street talk and wouldn't come off like some fucking nun in a convent.

Jeffie, who had liked the idea of Joey writing that book, got very excited about it and arranged for some limey, a writer named Donald, to talk to Joey. After Joey met him, he said he would be like a priest who knew shit about the street.

It was during all this that he chased Jeffie for good. The same day he got a moving van to take all her stuff back to California, he moved in with Sina and her daughter in the penthouse.

Over at Sina's one night he was telling me he didn't want any static from Jeffie till the divorce went through, that I'd have to fly to California to straighten it out if there was. The phone rang. It was Marta Orbach.

Punchy, next to me on the sofa, leaned over and asked, "What's she breaking his balls about now?"

"Who the fuck knows?" I said.

Joey was telling Marta, "Don't worry about it. I'll go right over. We'll get it back, don't worry." Then we heard Marta over the other end, so loud that Joey took the phone away from his ear. You couldn't hear what she was saying, except as a lot of buzzy yak-yak. "Fine, fine," said Joey. "Don't worry. Rely on me. We'll give her all the protection she wants."

As soon as he racked the phone, he said, "Let's go."

"Where we going?" I asked. "Who we giving all the protection?"

"Jerry will be meeting us downstairs in ten minutes. Then we're all going over to Mrs. Stone's apartment. Somebody put the snatch on her dog."

I said, "What the—" I looked at Punchy and he looked at me. "Let's go. Let's see what this is all about. What're we becoming, Ellery Queen over here?"

Sina came in and saw him in his peaked cap and leather jacket. She looked worried. I said, "It's nothing to be worried about. It's just a dog we're looking for."

That's when she looked at all three of us.

"Well, that's what we're looking for," I said.

Punchy ducked down behind me to keep from laughing. Joey was explaining Marta's call, that somebody had taken Mrs. Peter Stone's dog. She was alone, with her husband out of town, and she was a little afraid.

"Oh," said Sina, "that's the writer's wife."

Joey kissed her, then gave me a mild punch on the arm.

Marta's old man met us in the lobby. Driving over, Jerry Orbach was saying that this Mrs. Stone had gotten a call from someone who sounded like a junkie telling her that the dog was over in this hotel on West Forty-seventh Street. Joey said maybe it was a dognapping ring. Punchy and I couldn't even talk about it. How could you talk about a thing like that? There was Joey running to do favors. But a fucking dog, when every Colombo shooter was waiting to go on him, on all of us?

Mrs. Stone had a nice pad, a duplex. She was very elegant looking, all right, and there was Joey in the leather jacket and peaked cap, strutting around the living room, looking as serious as Jerry looked serious about that dog, and this broad going on about a reward she'd put in the papers, that the dog was gone for a couple of days, and about how dear the dog was to her. And Joey was doing the investigation—if they'd come in by the window, or they'd broken in the door, and where was it seen last, all that shit. I just couldn't believe it.

The woman had a real fine way of speaking and asked if we wanted coffee. "No, no, no coffee," said Joey. Then she asked if we'd like some wine. "Yeah," he said. "We'll have some wine."

Then, over the wine, she told about how she was impressed with him, how she looked forward to meeting him, and then about that dog, about the call she'd received from someone at a hotel on Forty-seventh Street, and she was going on about that.

"Listen," he told her, "if that's the area, I'll have the Greek get some of the guys to go down there, talk to the hotel manager to get some kind of a clue . . ."

I was listening to him talking, thinking to myself, here I am sitting with this guy, a broad that looks like a socialite, and Jerry Orbach, who's as serious about it as him, and they're talking about a fucking dog. Look at this guy. He goes from one extreme to the other. And here's this broad that's so impressed with him, and he's damned serious, when she doesn't even know him, will never know him, and she doesn't know what in the fuck she's getting herself into. She has to be crazier than him.

"Greek, listen," he said, "go down, get some of the guys. In fact, you know what you do? Call my nephew and have him come down with about four guys and meet you over on West Forty-seventh Street."

"Where on Forty-seventh?" I hated to even ask.

"Corner of Broadway. There's this hotel between Broadway and Seventh I want you guys to check. You have the address, Mrs. Stone?"

Her face was very bright. "Yes, I have it." She reached into her bag.

"Joey," I said, "you staying?" I didn't want to ask anything else.

Joey and Punchy were staying. Mrs. Stone, very bright and happy now, began describing the dog. I wasn't listening. It was enough that it was a dog.

On the corner of Broadway and Forty-seventh, I met Stevie Gallo with three other guys. Stevie wanted to know what was up, what was so important, and he started to say, "Greek, what're—"

I said, "Hey, listen, your uncle said we had to go over to that fleabag hotel over there, with all the fucking pimps and what not. Some guy put the snatch on a friend of Marta's dog."

"Dog!"

"Hey, leave me the fuck alone. You think I want to go in there? That's your uncle telling us to go. So let's make the attempt, some kind of fucking effort, and see if we can get a line on the guy who called about the dog, then get the fuck on home."

He was still looking at me like that.

"I know," I said, "I know," and walked ahead of them.

The hotel was grubby, hard lights, dirty floors with butts all over, and a windowed office like an old-style teller's cage. There we were, five guys in this all-black hotel, pimps with Afros taking one look and going far. At the cage I talked to the manager, as rough and grubby as the hotel, when this black chick, on the stairs, yelled, "Hey, baby. Got some money you want to spend?"

"Not the time for it right now," I said.

"But you is five fine-looking dudes. You looking for a little pleasure? Make your pleasure real good."

"We're on business, sweetheart."

"You ain't the man, are you?"

"We look like law?"

"You is either the law or them bad guys, one of the two."

"Well, we ain't the law."

"Then you must be them *bad* guys," she said.

I told the manager if he found the guy that called about a dog, for the reward, to give us a call, that there wouldn't be any problems. In fact, our friend might thank him personally with a little bread. Then he wanted to know what kind of dog. I told him, "You got to ask the guy that called."

Then I phoned Joey and told him, "Yeah, we're taking care of it. Everything is in process." Then, "Hey, Joey, this fucking dog. I'm going to get stoned after this. In fact, there's four more guys, including your nephew, who want to get stoned."

"Ah, go see your gummare."

"That's exactly what I'm going to do, go over to my gummare. At least with her, I get something. With you, I get nothing but a fucking headache, running around looking for a dog."

"Greek, I can't tell you what I want to tell you, 'cause there's a lady here."

"Well, fuck you too."

"Stay cool. See you tomorrow."

"Yeah," I said. "But do me a favor. Don't ask about no fucking dog."

fifteen

Almost a year to the day that Joey had come out of the slams, he married Sina over at Marta Orbach's townhouse. Marta, as usual, made all the arrangements. What was funny was that it included the minister who'd married Tiny Tim, and Allan Jones singing "The Lord's Prayer."

Joey wanted me at the wedding. I was working a paper score, some stocks and bonds, and Bobby Darrow had to be with me. A couple of things weren't going down right. When I explained it to him, he said to get the bread, but he wanted us to come by later for the reception.

Bobby and I tried the score, only it didn't come off. So we were tapped out, broke, and had nothing for the boost. You know, the Italian bridal gift of greens in the envelope. But we went to the reception anyway. Marta greeted us. I asked how everything went and talked and joked for a while, drinking champagne. A lot of Marta's friends were there, including David Steinberg.

Joey and Sina were in with a big circle of people,

and he looked happier than hell. I was very pleased
seeing him that happy for a change and hugged and
kissed him and Sina, congratulating them both. Then
he took me aside, asking if I'd scored.

"Don't ask," I said. "Nothing came off. So where
you going on your honeymoon? The Bahamas or something?"

"Get off that shit, Greek. Honeymoon."

"Yeah, pal, you've been honeymooning her for
quite a while now, haven't you?" I said.

Tony Bernardo had left, while Punchy moved
around like he was operating, looking for what he
could earn, what broad was around, what celebrity he
could score. The Mod Squad was coming by later, and
Punchy was staying. I told Joey that he probably
wanted to be alone with his new bride, congratulated
him again, and left. We hadn't been there more than
an hour.

A couple of days later Joey had us going with
him over to Mulberry Street to Joe the Wop's place
and to Luna's Restaurant, then wiseguy hangouts.
There was no sense telling him that the minute we got
there it would be all over the street, but I told him
anyway.

"What're you worried about?" he said.

I gave him one of those looks.

He liked Luna's. Don't ask me why. He'd been
busted there a couple of times. We never stayed
around too long, but sometimes we'd go across the
street to Joe the Wop's, see guys like Frankie the Bug*
and Joe Curly,† but mostly we were there to see
Georgie Argenda, who owed Blast some greens. He
didn't look very happy with us coming around. He
expected shots to go off.

Georgie Argenda, a big guy, was the one who
gave Joey the lion that time. He'd give monkeys, ba-
boons, things like that, as gifts, and he had given Joey
the lion as a cub during the Profaci war. After we'd
gone into Joe the Wop's the first time, I told Joey that

_____
*Frank Caruso.
†Joseph Argone.

the only thing missing from his wedding was that lion and Armando the Dwarf.

Toward the end of March, only about two weeks after Joey's marriage, Darrow and I picked him up at the penthouse. In the car, he told me to get over to President Street. I asked, "What route you want me to take this time? Brooklyn Bridge, Manhattan, what? Take the tunnel, or stay out of the tunnel?"

"Go any fucking way you want to go. Just go."

"Oh, you're in one of those moods," I said. "Whatsamatter? Your new wife giving you a hard time already?" I started to laugh.

"Greek, stop breaking balls."

"Hey," I said, "I've had my fill of marriages too, you know. But I'm very happy now. All you've got to do is find yourself, Jim."

"Don't give me none of that Jim-shit jive talk. Just get me the fuck over to President."

"You got it, boss."

"And don't give me none of that boss shit. Understand?"

"Okay. Let's go."

I took the Brooklyn Bridge. It was still raining, a miserable drizzle. We were halfway over when I saw a license plate with the numbers 303. Joey saw it too. He wasn't so down after that. That was his lucky number. He said he was going to lay a C-note on it in the morning.

Over at Dolly's we saw ourselves curved and long in that round convex mirror attached outside. Jimmy Springs had checked us out in the mirror. It seemed that everyone was gone. Joey looked at Jimmy and said, "Pegleg, where is everybody?"

"The funeral," said Jimmy Springs.

"What funeral?"

"Joey Balzano's uncle."

"Yeah? Who went?"

"Your brother, lot of the guys. Joey, it's Colombo territory."

"No kidding? Enough guys go?"

"Plenty."

Something was working on Joey, and I asked, "What're you thinking? What're you up to?"

"Ah, let's get something to eat, some pasta or something," he said.

Over at the Queen Restaurant we ate and had a bottle of wine, but all along you just knew something was working on Joey. He kept circling his fork on his plate, smearing what was left of the sauce and pasta. Then he said, "Let's shake 'em up."

"Here it comes," I said. "Shake *who* up?"

He smiled.

"Forget it," I said.

"The Colombos will have to show their respect."

"Hey, come on. You serious?"

"Balzano's uncle is a button. Everybody'll be there," he said.

After he found out that the funeral parlor was along New Utrecht Avenue, and I'd heard it was near Eighty-sixth Street, practically next door to the Colombos, I asked Joey, "How we going?"

"How you mean 'going'?"

"I mean, just two pieces, or a machine gun and a cannon? Listen, why don't we just go over to Joe Colombo's house? Hey, let's think about it. Blast is already there at the funeral with a bunch of the guys. You and your brother together up there, with a lot of Colombos?"

"You packing?"

"Joey."

"Bobby?"

"Stashed," said Darrow.

"Get it."

"Guess you thought about it," I said.

We found the funeral parlor at the intersection of Bath and New Utrecht avenues, right under the el. A lot of cars were out front. We made no law. I said, "Listen, there's an ashcan on the outside. Want to dump the pieces there? Let's not keep 'em in the fucking car in case when we come out, there's law and they want to tackle the car and us at the same time."

"Get them in the ashcan," said Joey.

Bobby Darrow snapped open the plastic bag he had just for that, saying who wanted the pistols picking up coffee grounds and putrid fish.

"Listen, we'll circle the block," I said. "Bobby, you walk, dump the pieces in the can at the far end over there, so at least we'll know where they're at, while we park the car in front. Then when we leave, you get the pieces, walk two blocks down. We'll pick you up. But if you make law or we make them, we'll give you two honks on the horn, and you just keep walking. Forget them fucking pieces. You got that?"

He had the two pistols, folding the plastic bag over them like he was wrapping a sandwich, saying, "Hey, you keep talking to me like it's my first time, Greek."

After I'd parked, we waited for Bobby to catch up. Then when we all went in, the smell of the flowers hit. Further inside we saw the coffin with lights behind it and flowers all around, and chairs and a lot of people in black. Then they saw us. You never saw so many big eyeballs. Blast had the biggest stunned look of all. I made at least five Colombos huddled together, and there were more of them in another group. Counting ourselves, there were at least fifteen Gallos, as well as guys from different crews. The Colombos stared, then turned away.

Joey went along shaking hands. You could feel those Colombos watching us as we went along. Joey paid his respects to the Balzano kid and his family. He didn't even look at the coffin. Then he said to the kid, "Your uncle was all right. A good fella. But he died, he's dead, what the hell. Think only he lived a good life. Don't mourn over here. *Buona salute.*"

"*Buona salute,*" said Balzano.

There were some guys that worked at the Copa paying their respects. You could still feel the Colombos eyeing us. I saw one turning away. I'd made him as one of the guys I'd seen at Colombo's funeral home when Mimi Scialo's mother passed away.

Joey was talking to some people and I was shaking hands with somebody else when that same Colombo came by. I knew him from Abby, but I'd forgotten his name. It was as though he wasn't looking at me when he said, "Hi, Greek."

"Hi," I said, and I wasn't looking at him either.

"Seems the only time we meet is at funerals," he said.

"Yeah," I said, and moved away.

About two years before, Blast and I had been called down to see Colombo and the big don himself, Carlo Gambino. They'd made it clear that they only wanted to see the two of us, and the hell of it was the meet was to be at the funeral parlor. It looked like a Profaci special—the nice conversation, then turkey time, and off we'd go in the false bottoms of Colombo's coffins.

So we went packing, insult or no insult, taking five guys with us. There we were, paying our respects to Mimi Scialo's relatives, and not thinking about that at all, when Mooney, who had made all the arrangements, came over with a sour face. I said, "Yeah, Doc?"

"The old man and Joe C will see you now."

Joe Colombo and Carlo Gambino, along with a couple of their people, were sitting around in the office when we came in. It was the first time we'd met the old man. Colombo made the introductions, saying, "This is my gumbaro, Carlo." Gambino had a nice, quiet way about him, spoke with a slight accent, but a clear voice.

The old man knew I ran Greek Town, and it seemed that a lot of goods from his sons' trucks around there were being ripped off. He wanted to know if I had any word on boosters who'd been working his sons' trucks, and said he wanted it stopped. He told me to give the word nice, no rough stuff. If it didn't stop, then he would have to take a different approach. I said certainly, I'd see to it. Then he reminded me to be nice, not to cause trouble.

Gambino was smiling and pleasant all along, but the smile left him when he went to get his vicuna coat. Somebody had stolen it.

There was this rough, all-black café near Greek Town and I knew this one big guy. I told him somebody was boosting stuff from the wrong trucks, gave the names of the companies, but nothing else, only that they belonged to strong people, very strong, and that touching them was a serious mistake. There would be no consequences once it stopped. I guess I told the right guy because it stopped the next day.

The old man was grateful, but a lot of wiseguys resented it that I, a Greek, had talked to him directly, that he had preferred seeing me face to face.

sixteen

On the night of Joey's birthday, April 6, I picked up my gummare, Edith Russo, and drove to Joey's apartment. On the way Edith had been all too quiet, and I said, "Whatsamatter?"

"Nothing."

"What do you mean, nothing? You haven't said a word."

"How long has Joey been home?"

"Don't know. About thirteen months. Something like that."

"That's all? It's more like thirteen years."

"That what you've been thinking?"

"No," she said, "not that," and she went quiet again.

I guess she'd been wondering about my wife. It wasn't a subject I ever discussed with her, other than that I was married and had kids. She'd ask about the kids, how they were, that kind of thing, and say that my wife must have been an especially nice woman. I'd say she was, and let it go at that.

Edith was a hell of a fine girl—young, only in her

twenties—and I suppose I liked her as much as I possibly could. It wasn't only that she was pretty, or good in the sack. That wasn't all there was to her. She was really very nice to be around, and not coming on like most other gummares who were out to get all they could from some wiseguy, going for the mink coat and all that crap. She never asked for anything or made any kinds of demands on you. It wouldn't have done her any good if she had.

She seemed worried for some reason, then she tried to smile. Bobby Darrow said, "What the hell. It's going to be one hell of a night."

"Yes," said Edith, brightening.

"Hey, Bobby," I said. "Call your gummare. Bring her along."

"To hell with my gummare," he said.

I suddenly didn't like the word "gummare," hearing it or saying it. I looked over at Edith. She was really smiling now.

When we got up to the penthouse, Edith and Sina embraced, saying nice things to each other. Sina's daughter, Lisa, stood looking at us, wearing Joey's peaked cap, her hands on her hips, an unlit cigarette in her mouth. I had to remind myself that she was only a kid, maybe ten at most.

"Light me up," she said.

Just then Joey came out of the bedroom. "Come here, tough guy," he said to her, lighting a match.

Cam, Joey's sister, said that was awful—giving Lisa cigarettes. Then she asked me about the wife and kids. I was glad Edith hadn't heard it. I told her they were fine, that they had gone to the country. She was smiling but she seemed a little fidgety looking over at Edith.

Cam had short blonde hair and looked a little like Joey, but she wasn't all that pretty. She was a widow, and sometimes she could get very emotional, and could be very hard to handle. It turned out she was visiting Joey, and he had invited her to come along with us to the Copa.

Joey asked if I'd called the Copa for a table.

"Sure, I called them," I said, then kidded him

about wearing decent threads for a change, a nice pin-stripe suit, and not his usual leather jacket and cap. We all had a drink together. Then Joey asked if we were ready to go. "Sure," I said.

We made it for the second show and sat at the long table on the top terrace, having champagne and Chinese food. Don Rickles worked over Jews, blacks, and Italians, but only certain Italians, not the Italians that were there. He said he wanted to make that clear. Then, with those eyes and that grin of his, he gave a "Hi" up to our table. Then another "Hi," saying, "I was told to be *very* careful what I said, particularly to those people on the upper balcony on the left-hand side of me." That brought a laugh. Joey held up an empty champagne bottle as though he would throw it. Rickles covered his head with his arms, yelling, "Ma! Ma!" That brought a bigger laugh.

About then the manager sent over champagne. So did the Orbachs and their bunch. Punchy and his gum-mare were with them, along with Earl Wilson, the column writer, and some women. Marta came over and told Joey he should have told her that it was his birth-day, that she would have given him a party. Joey said, "My boys are right here. They're taking good care of me."

After the show we all went to the lounge and had drinks at the round bar. The girls sat at the table talk-ing among themselves. Champagne was still being sent over. A wiseguy named Frank sent some. He was with an old-timer, Russ Bufalino, a regular greaseball, the boss of Erie, Pennsylvania. Joey, feeling no pain with all the champagne, grinned at the button in Bufalino's lapel. It was a Colombo "Numero Uno" button with a diamond in it. "Hey," said Joey, "what're you doing with that? You really believe in that bullshit league?"

You saw how Bufalino's chin went, his back going very straight, turning away from us. Frank, with a very worried look, took Joey by the arm. "Joey, that's nothing to talk about here. Let's just have a few drinks."

"Yeah, we'll have a few drinks."

"Joey, he's a boss."

"So he's a boss. So am I a boss. That make him any better than me? We're all equal. We're all supposed to be brothers." "Brothers" came out like it was anything but.

"Joey," I said, "let's go to the table. Let's not have a beef."

At the table in the lounge with the girls, Edith asked what was wrong. I said, "Nothing. We're all having a good time."

I don't think Joey would have dropped it, but Don Rickles came over just then with his mother. He talked about the old Elegante in Brooklyn. Joey asked him if he remembered the time he shot up the place. "Remember it?" said Rickles. "How can I forget it? Now every time you come in, I don't know what the fuck to do, whether to duck under the table or run off the stage."

They talked for almost an hour. All the while Bobby was rapping with some broad. Bobby whispered in my ear, smelling of booze, "I'm cutting out with her."

"Wait a minute. You're not cutting out no place. Didn't we talk about this, that when we're on him, we've got to stay with Joey? You want to bang her? Fine. But after we drop him off."

"Whatsamatter?" asked Joey. "Stiff prick Bob wants to take on big boobies there? Let him get laid."

"Fine. But are you going right home?"

"Ah, let's have something to eat."

"We just ate."

"Yeah, but the girls are still hungry," he said. "Let's go someplace."

When we got to the car, he was still insistent about getting something to eat. Bobby and the broad were standing off to the side. "Go with the broad," Joey told him.

"That's a mistake," I said. "I'm telling you."

"Ah, he wants to put that stiff dick in her. If I don't let him, his face'll be hanging."

Bobby and the girl headed off, looking for a taxi. I didn't like it at all. I began to get bad feelings.

Joey wanted to go down to Chinatown and eat, and I said, "We just ate Chinese food, didn't we?" But he wanted Chinese food, wanted to go to Su Ling's. It was closed. Other restaurants were open, but he wanted Su Ling's. Then he decided on Luna's.

"Luna's you want to go and eat at? Of all places, you pick Luna's. Too many guys have made us going to Luna's and Joe the Wop's. Joey, let's head on home."

"Luna's," he said, talking to Sina and his sister, and I was giving him my one eye real good. "Luna's, Greek," he said.

It was shut and dark when we drove up. "Good," I said. "Let's head home."

But then, as we came around to Mulberry and Hester streets, there on the corner, arches and square windows all lit up, was a brand new place called Umberto's Clam House. Outside I made Matty the Horse* and Joe Pesh,† looking as though something had happened. Joey told me, "Stop here."

"Joey, let's get on home."

"Ask how the food is."

"That's Matty the Horse, and Joe Pesh, a guy you don't know."

"Ask them."

Matty the Horse, a capo in the Genovese Family, was the big fat guy. Joe Pesh ran numbers. "Pesh" meant fish, and he was almost as big, but had a neck on him like a fat bull.

Matty looked to make us when the car pulled up. I rolled down the window. "Hi, Matty," I said.

"Hey, how are you, Pete?"

"All right. Who's place is this?"

"My brother's."

"Food any good?"

"Good. Very good," he said.

Joey wanted me to park. I told him, "Let's get out of here."

"Pull around the corner, find a place to park."

"Joey, don't you understand?"

---

*Matthew Ianniella.
†Joseph Luparelli.

"Hey, Greek, stop breaking balls. The girls are hungry. Girls, don't you want some seafood?"

They said they did, except Edith, who was watching me. Cam said Umberto's looked like a nice place. I said it wasn't so nice.

I went once around the block. There was an opening in front of Umberto's like it had been made for us. I parked.

Inside there were people at the tables, a few at the counter. I checked for the doors, the one we'd come in and the other at the far right, where we took a table. I put myself between Joey and the side door. The side door was the one to worry about.

A worse feeling hit me. It must have hit Joey too. After we ordered, he said he was going to check downstairs. I said we'd both check.

"Stay with them, and no arguments," he told me.

All the while Cam had been watching us. She had a very worried look about her now. After a while she said, "Pete, he's been down there too long."

"Don't worry. He's just down to the john."

"But he's been there too long."

"You're uptight, you know that, Cam? Relax. I'll go down."

He was at the foot of the staircase, looking around. There was no way out. When we started up, he just stopped. "Greek," he said.

"Whatsamatter?"

"Ah, come on. Let's go up and eat," he said.

The food was on the table. While we ate, the girls talked about the show at the Copa. Joey brought up Don Rickles at the old Elegante and said that Rickles had come a long way. I made Matty the Horse at the counter behind us sitting with a big pimply-faced guy. The girls were still talking among themselves. Lisa looked a little sleepy, but Cam still had that look.

I made that pimply-faced guy still at the counter. Matty the Horse moved off for the kitchen. Just then, at the side door, I saw Sonny Pinto,* wide and dark, coming in. I began to tell Joey when everything started

*Carmine Di Biase.

hitting inside me, the blood pounding, hearing Sonny scream, "Motherfucker!"

A shot went off. Joey and I threw the table up, Sonny firing shots right for our faces, then other shots, something slamming me to the floor, not knowing how I got there, only that I was down, and everything going off all at once, bottles exploding, plates spinning and breaking, metal clanging, everybody screaming, going for the floor or running.

Then everything stopped. It just stopped. I didn't see Joey anywhere, but a lot of blood, broken glasses, and overturned chairs, and people all over the floor. I had a burning hot rush when I tried to stand. Matty the Horse was on the floor in the kitchen, his hands covering the back of his head. The scalding rush went all through the left side of me. Going out the side door, I saw them running.

I made Sonny Pinto and two other guys. I had the piece out and threw the bolt, a shell flipping out. I held it as steady as I could, squeezing off a round for the sonofabitch's head, firing again, and they were scrambling, firing back, that white cement of Umberto's sparking, chipping all around me. I kept firing at the bastards. I knew I hit something before their car turned off, screeching hard. I'd emptied and had nothing left.

Everything was hitting me. Back inside I looked for Joey. A lot of people and stuff were on the floor. Nobody was moving. Matty had gone for the kitchen. He had to be in on it. He had to know. In the kitchen, there was that fat sonofabitch on the floor still with his hands covering his head.

I jammed the piece against his fucking ear. "Get up, you motherfucker! Get up!"

"Pete!"

"You had everything to do with this!"

"No, Pete! I swear! Nothing!" He was whining, screaming almost.

"Get up! Get *up!* Get up before I blow your fucking head off right here!"

I had him by the back of the collar, the piece jammed against his head, pushing him out in front of me, pushing him as hard as I could. Everything scalded. When I had him in the dining room, I saw blood all around Edith, and I said, "My Christ." I saw her head coming up, and it wasn't blood at all, but all that sauce from the bottles. You could still smell the shots, smoke was still hanging. "Edith, you all right?" She nodded. She was in shock. They were all in shock. Sina was over on top of Lisa. "Is everybody all right?" I yelled.

I didn't see Joey anywhere. Then, through the front window, I made him on his back in the middle of the street. My heart went hard. I shoved Matty, going out to him, saying, "Oh, my God."

Cam was bent down over him, hysterical. He was breathing hard, rasping. I yelled for somebody to call an ambulance. People just kept looking. I was screaming at them. Nobody moved. I wanted to kill them. I wanted to kill somebody.

Then a sector car pulled up. I also saw the big pimply-faced guy watching us. I flipped off the piece before this one cop came over, asking what happened.

"Never mind what happened!" I yelled. "Get him to the hospital!"

"Who is he? He looks familiar."

"It's my brother Joey Gallo, Joe Gallo!" wailed Cam.

"Get him to the hospital! He's dying!" I screamed.

I picked Joey up and got him to the back of the police car. Cam pushed herself right in after us, screaming. I gave Joey mouth-to-mouth. Breathe, Joey! Breathe! Then I had him going, and all the while the cops were asking questions and I wasn't saying a fucking word to them, just trying to get Joey going, and he was. He was breathing easier. I really had him going right by the time we got to Beekman Hospital.

In the emergency room, they closed the door. "You're not closing the door on him!" I yelled. Then I saw them working him with electric shocks, seeing him jolt, then jolt again. Then they just stopped, and that long, steady squeal. The doctor didn't have to tell me, he didn't have to tell me anything. Joey was dead. I started screaming that they could still do some-

thing, cut open his chest, massage his heart, anything.
But the doctor said he was gone, and he took me by
the arm. "Get over here," he said. "Sit down. You're
shot."

"I'm not shot."

"You're shot, I'm telling you."

I was looking up at the hard lights, the stiff white
sheet under me, and everything smelling of the hospital. I was shot twice, they said, and I was saying
where. The cop started to question me and I yelled,
"Get the fuck away from me!"

They had me on a stretcher waiting for X-rays
when I saw Blast standing over me. "Greek, who was
it?" Then he came with his ear to my mouth.

"Sonny Pinto," I whispered. "Two other guys."

He stood. Nothing changed in him. Roy-Roy and
Papa Gallo were standing off.

Papa Gallo squeezed my shoulder. His eyes were
watery. "Pete, you all right?"

"Yeah, Papa. I'm all right." My eyes were watery
too.

They went out behind the white curtain.

They found that the bullet had gone clean through
my hip and out the side of my leg. My wrist had been
bandaged, and I asked if I'd been hit there too.

Someone said, "Don't you know?"

I looked at my wrist, then let my arm go down.

They were wheeling me back to the emergency
room, the ceiling lights and turns making me feel dizzy.
I wouldn't close my eyes. I could still see the gun
flashes in my face.

seventeen

After they moved me up to a room, all sorts of hospital people kept coming in. One doctor asked how I was feeling. I told him, "All right," and he said, "Well, you shouldn't be." A nurse stuck a cold thermometer in my mouth that tasted of alcohol, while a cop stood off with his hands in his pockets.

Then I was left alone. Sometimes I could hear people talking outside my door. I didn't know if they were cops or what. One guy said I was one lucky sonofabitch, that over twenty shots had gone off in and out of the place, and the guy that shot me had to have been a lousy shot or drunk. "Yeah," said the other, sounding as though it was all very funny.

It kept going through my head. It wasn't even seconds. It was fast, very fast. But there had been three shooters, maybe one with two pieces, shots on top of shots, and then that last, the final, and everything just hanging before I could even move. Maybe they thought they had me dead when I dropped, maybe with all the busted bottles of red sauce around me, Edith, and everyone else. I had thought she was dead and everyone else too.

I'd only made Sonny Pinto letting go, then I knew it had been three when I made the other two running with him for the car. Knew I hit something twice, at least twice. I wasn't all that sure if I'd clipped one of them or the car. Maybe one of the tires. Well, they weren't going so far if the car had bullet holes in it, and maybe a flat.

Somebody had called or had gone running to tell them we were at Umberto's. Maybe from the phone in the kitchen. Somebody dropped the dime. Maybe Matty the Horse or that Joe Pesh went running. Pesh wasn't around after we'd parked out front. It could have been him or Matty who'd dropped the dime, or they both were in on it.

All the times we were on Mulberry Street, at Luna's or Joe the Wop's, they could have taken us off the right way, not cowboying it with women and a kid around. But Bobby Darrow had always been with us. That made three, so the odds weren't so good for them. Still, they could have taken us off anywhere they wanted: in a joint, coming out, or blocking the car off at the corner, then letting go.

It had to be that the Colombos, knowing we were coming around there, had given it to some different crew to set it up on Mulberry Street, just as Joe Colombo had set us up with Chin when he wanted Joey and Blast taken off that time. They just waited for their opportunity, for somebody to eyeball us.

Sonny Pinto. I'd even staked him when he came out of the slams for murder. He was no big earner or mover, and he was doing work for Matty the Horse. Sober he was nothing, but drunk he'd blow your head off. He must have been sauced, and there it was five in the morning, later even, and he must have been in some afterhours joint, sauced, playing cards, either into a big game of ziganette or blackjack, or shooting dice, when that call came or somebody came running.

I was putting everything together. Joe Pesh out in front of Umberto's, then disappearing. Matty the

Horse and that big fat guy with pimples talking at the counter, right behind us, like they were posting themselves where we were. Then Matty going for the kitchen just before the comeoff, when Pinto walked in. Then afterward, when I was over Joey in the middle of the street, that pimply-face big guy standing off, watching, as though he wanted to make sure Joey was dead.

There it was, a combo. It had to be that. It couldn't be anything else. Matty, at least, had to know the comeoff. Pinto owed the big obligation. Matty had helped him when he'd gone on the lam after being sentenced to the chair for murder. Matty had paid the big attorney fees to get Pinto off on the technicality. He owed the big obligation not only for that but for work he was doing for Matty, and he couldn't have come into Matty's place before the shooting without having told him first. So Matty the Horse had to be in on it. He had to.

All right, they loaded up and they killed Joey. They must have been told he was there with his wife and sister, and his stepdaughter, a kid. If Darrow had been with us, they might have cooled it. The only thing that might have stopped them was another shooter with us, not people and a little kid. Nothing was about to stop them, not some people or a kid they might have killed. They moved like fucking animals. All they cared about was killing Joey. Well, they killed him. That's all I cared about now. I just couldn't sleep. I could still see Joey's dead body.

"Greek?" I heard somebody say in my mind. Then I heard it again. It was Larry Gallo, and I had to think about that too, the time he was at St. Vincent's Hospital, after the operation for cancer, and there he was sitting up with the fever blanket around him, shivering. "Where's Joey?" he'd asked.

"He's coming," I told him. "He said he'd come and he'll come."

He kept listening for him, but when Joey came in, he looked away as though he hadn't been listening at all. Joey, seeing him with the blanket and the shakes, said, "What're you shaking for?" Larry said it wasn't him; it was the bed. Then Joey started kidding him, telling him to get the old lady in the sack with him, to keep him warm, like Jane Russell in *The Outlaw*.

They were still talking when I left the room. After that Larry's spirits were way up. Joey had one hell of an effect on him. Well, they really loved each other, and for a while it looked as though Larry would make it. But he wasn't making anything. He was dying hard and he knew he was dying.

Then one of the last times I saw him and I was alone with him, he said, "Greek, I want to ask you a question. Not a question. I'm going to tell you something to do. I'm going to tell you and you got to do it for me."

"Larry, whatever I can do for you, I'll do it."

"But if I tell you, you got to do it. You're not going to tell me anything else."

"If I tell you I will, I'll do it."

"Tomorrow when you come up here, bring a pistol. Leave it with me."

"Larry."

"Do as I tell you."

All the while he was hardly able to talk with all the pain. Then he came on tough, "You understand me, Greek?"

"I can't answer you."

"Don't get me fucking aggravated. If I tell you to do something, you got to do it. Remember, I'm the fucking boss over here."

"Okay, Larry. That's what you want? That's what I'll do."

"Don't just say that to pacify me. Bring it. It's costing too much keeping me here. I'm not going to survive this fucking thing. I know it."

"Okay."

"Bring it, Greek. Bring it."

"All right, Larry, I'll bring it," I said.

But that was the one thing I couldn't do. I couldn't even have done that for Joey. There was always the chance Larry could survive. But there was no chance for him. He died hard, suffering. Christ, I had to remember all that. Now both brothers were dead.

In the morning I was booked on a gun charge. I was being held on fifty thousand dollars' bail. My lawyer called to say he was trying to make arrangements with my associates and to lower the bail. The DA's people wanted a statement. I told them I had nothing to say. Then came two feds. The one named Quinn asked how I felt, then said, "You got caught short."

"Yeah, we did get caught short."

"Shame."

"Yeah."

"Don't imagine you want to discuss it with us."

I saw the other smile.

"No," I said, "rather not discuss it."

"Well, if there's anything we can do."

"No, thanks, but I appreciate that."

The smile went wider on the other.

"You were lucky," said Quinn. "Damned sure were. Well, take good care of yourself."

"You too," I said.

Then I was moved to another room. I don't know why, but I was. Two cops were kept outside. I was arraigned, fingerprinted, and mugged. I wouldn't sign the fingerprint card. A detective, who happened to be a Greek, said it was only procedure, that I couldn't make bail without signing. I called my lawyer and he said to sign it. I told the detective in Greek I was only signing it because he was a countryman.

My wife, who had been with the kids out of town at her sister's, had heard the news bulletins that Joey had been killed. She thought I'd been killed alongside him. When she learned I was at Beekman, she had her brother drive her right over. She was crying hysterically. I tried calming her but it wasn't any good. I kept telling her I was all right, but she couldn't stop shaking and crying.

"Listen," I said, "I'm all right. All right. Calm down. Come on, now. Sit down, sit down. Come on, babe."

She was still shaking. I took her hands and you could feel that tremor all through her. I said, "Hey, I think you need the bed next to me."

"I do. I do. You don't know what you've put me through. You have no idea."

"Babe, I'm sorry," I said, and I felt lousy.

Then my father visited—strong, straight up, graying, a trim mustache—but it was pretty much the same thing, with him crying too. He wanted to know if I was all right, that was all he wanted to know. Then he said he'd buy me an airline ticket and send me to Greece, that I should go, that this was no life for me. My wife agreed with him. It made me feel even lousier.

After my father left, my wife stayed till well into the afternoon. I told her to get on home to the kids, that it made no sense hanging around. She just looked at that bottle hanging next to the bed and the hose that led to my arm, and asked if that's how they were feeding me, intravenously. When I said yes, she said she would ask the doctors if I could get something decent to eat, that it couldn't taste very good going through my arm. I told her to make sure the kids got no wind of this, to keep the TV off at news time, and to keep the papers away from the kids.

"You know I'll do that."

"Yeah, I know," I said. "Better get on home."

"First I'll get you something decent to eat," she said.

Later that afternoon the cop held the door open with the flat of his hand, saying, "Know this guy?"

It was Bobby Darrow.

"No," I said, "don't know him. Send him in."

"Know him or don't you?" asked the cop.

"I know him," I said.

Darrow, grinning, was sauced out of his head. He was all the way over like the Tower of Pisa, the way he always did when he was sauced. I sat up, the tube almost pulling out of my arm, stinging. "Shut the door," I told the cop.

"Jesus, pal," said Darrow, "how you feeling?"

"Come here. Get close to me. Get real close to me."

He stopped. "Whatsamatter?"

"Whatsamatter? I tell you whatsamatter." And I started cursing, yelling at him that he thought more of a broad than he did of Joey, leaving us like that to get suckered. Joey was dead. Did he understand that? Joey was dead. And I would have climbed all over him, only that tube was taped to my arm. He kept backing away, saying it wasn't his fault, that he felt as bad about it as I did, felt bad that I'd been shot too.

"Get away from me!" I yelled.

"Why do you think I'm smashed?"

"You get smashed for any reason, any reason at all. You're all fucked up with uppers, downers, and all the booze you can shove down your throat, and you got us fucked up."

"But Joey said it was all right."

"Joey's *dead!* Understand that? He's dead! Now just get the fuck away from me!"

"All right."

"Get away!"

"I'm going."

"Right now! Get the fuck out of here, *now!* I want no part of you!"

"All right, all right."

He backed away till he got to the door.

The following day two guys from Greek Town came to see me. One was Little Georgie, my partner in one of the clubs, and Louie, a fat guy who was just a friend. Georgie told me that Bobby Darrow had stopped at the club last night and had abused him and Louie, saying that he needed a thousand dollars right away for me, that they had to get it up, and he didn't care how they got it.

"You gave it to him?"

"Well, sure," said Georgie. "I went and got it, 'cause I thought it was important that you needed it."

"Listen to me, the two of you. The next time he comes to the club—shoot him. Hear what I'm telling you? You got a gun up there? Right? Shoot him. If you don't shoot him, I'll shoot the two of you."

"Pete."

"He's crazy. He's out of his fucking mind. He's

drinking, taking pills. I don't know what he'll do next."

Georgie took a long look at me. "So what's the matter with him?"

"I told you. And I'm telling you what to do. Now you do as I tell you."

"All right," said Little Georgie, "so long as you're telling us. Now we know what to do."

Bail was lowered to five thousand. Here I was, under arrest and wounded, and the word Blast got back to me was he would try to get the security up. But a day went by and he hadn't gotten up anything. The only one who called at all was Roy-Roy, who asked if I needed anything.

My wife arranged to bring food and beer, and I had the cops eat with us. She'd go quiet when they were around. She was still pretty upset, particularly about Blast not coming through. Then she started in again about getting out of town, going someplace, anyplace. I told her there was still a little problem of making bail, then facing this trial, to see what was coming out of it. I talked to her about the fucked-up life I was living, maybe I'd get out of it, maybe make it easier for her and the kids. I saw the way she looked at me. I said, "First I have to get out of this. The kids know about this yet?"

"God no."

"Good. I don't want them to know. I don't want them to ever know," I said. "Listen, babe, think your mother could help me over here? I mean, put some money up?"

"I don't know."

"Well, doesn't she have anything salted away?"

"Well, she's got some savings."

"Christ, babe, I hate to ask this, but do you think she could put it up so I can make bail?"

"Well, I'll ask her."

"Babe, I really hate to say this, but will you?" I felt lousy.

It took my mother-in-law twenty minutes to put up her bankbook so I could make bail. The only hitch was that the hospital people wanted to keep me under observation for a few more days. A doctor, with a thick mustache and his breath smelling of Listerine, said that although the bullet had gone clean through, there was still the possibility that some foreign substance or bits of clothing had gotten into my wound, and they wanted to make sure that no infection was setting in. I agreed to stay a couple of more days.

My lawyers, Bob Weiswasser and his brother Howard, along with Tony Bernardo, wanted to move me out at night, thinking there would be less chance of running into reporters. But the night I was to leave, Bob Weiswasser, bringing over some of my things to the bed, said, "There's a bunch of them out there, looking to break balls as usual, looking to get a statement."

"Yeah, I'll give them a statement," I said, flicking my hand under my chin.

I tried putting my weight on my bad leg, holding my hip when I moved. He passed over my coat. Tony Bernardo was standing off. "Where's Joey laid out?" I asked him.

"On Clinton."

"Well, I want to see him," I said.

The two lawyers backed away.

When we came out, going for the car, there was a pack of reporters and photographers elbowing in, the reporters yelling questions at me. I tried pulling my coat over my head as flashbulbs began exploding. It was like the gunshot flashes at Umberto's all over again.

eighteen

At Guido's Funeral Home, Joey was in his coffin. It stunned me. It had stunned everyone. I felt bad for his family, seeing Mama Gallo and his sisters in black, all broken up. Papa Gallo was just sitting there, his eyes watery, his chin quivering. I never felt so goddamned sad in my life.

Sina and her daughter were there, the Orbachs, and the crew. Jeffie and her daughter weren't there. After spending all those hard, grieving years with Joey, she deserved that right far more than Sina.

People shook hands with me, saying things, but I wasn't listening. Some of the crew embraced me, asking how the hip felt, and I said all right, looking not at them but at Joey.

I took a seat with my wife, her head and arm on my shoulder. Then I saw Bobby Darrow wrecked out of his mind. My stomach went tight. There he was in a brand new suit, one of four that he'd bought with the thou he'd ripped off Little Georgie. But to see that it didn't seem to matter to him that Joey was in his coffin, that really got me disgusted.

157

I thought of the time Joey told us if we ever got suckered, he wouldn't shed a fucking tear, and there he was in his coffin after getting suckered like a fucking idiot, right in their own backyard.

All right. Here was a guy that was wild. They called him Crazy Joe. No, he wasn't crazy. He just wouldn't take anybody's shit. But when he did something, no matter what it was, even hitting a guy, it was done the right way, by the greaseball laws, by their regulations, and by their rules. And, despite what anyone thought of him, he never once took a guy off in front of his kid or his wife. A guy that does is an animal. And Joey, because of the laws he lived by, never would have believed that it could happen in front of a kid and his wife.

The old greasers had a lot of pride, and they had respect. They never would have made a hit like this. When they did it, it was the right way. Sonny Pinto, American-born, changed all the rules.

Just then Blast stood, came up next to me with his hands clasped. He bent down to whisper. "Kitty, excuse me," he said to my wife. Then he whispered, "We have to have a talk later, pertaining to what happened."

"Yeah," I said, "we'll talk."

Louie the Syrian turned in his chair. Whatever he wanted to say to me, he didn't. He was taking it as bad as I was. I just kept looking at Joey.

"Kitty, go on home," I said. "Go on."

Her head came off my shoulder. "All right."

"I'll be by later. Just want to stay a little longer."

Some were leaving the funeral home, Joey's family too. That baby face of Stevie Gallo's was very sad. "Listen," I said to him, "whoever's left, let them get out. Leave me alone with him."

Everyone was gone. They closed the door. There was nothing left now but the empty rows of chairs, the flowers, the coffin. I went down the aisle to him, then just stood looking down, remembering a lot of things.

Shit.

Joey was just a little blond-haired runt of twelve when he got into a fight with some guy outside the schoolyard of P.S. 179 on Avenue C, right by some two-family houses with the flower pots on the sills. The guy was a lot bigger and they were really going at it. I was about to step in and help Joey, give the other guy a clout, when Joey said, "Just lay back. Don't worry about it, kid."

"Kid?" I said, and I wanted to give him a shot, the cocky little bastard.

They were right by a porch and a woman came out yelling. Joey reached up, grabbed a flower pot, and came right down on the guy's head. The woman screamed, the pot shattered, and the guy was out.

I just looked at him and said, "Nice." Then I told Joey, "You'd better get out of here," so we headed along, and he said, "Thanks a lot for wanting to help. But I wasn't in any trouble or I'd have got you to give him a kick. What's your name?"

He had me smiling, a little runt like that. I said, "Pete. I know your name—Joey. I've seen you around."

"Yeah?" He was shaking his hand. "Stings," he said. "Stung when I hit him."

"Well, the guy's head must sting a lot more," I said.

That was how it all started, just palling around with him and Mike the Bandit at the candy store on Thirty-sixth and Fourteenth Avenue, along with Frankie Illiano, before he got the name of Punchy.

We talked about taking off that warehouse where they kept Studebaker parts, but Joey and I decided not to go in on it. Mike and some other kids took it off. Only a week afterward they were all caught when this kid, trying to peddle parts, was picked up.

Joey and I talked about going on a few things, but he never went. He was already moving with older guys. Don't think I was more than thirteen when I got into robbing houses with some kids. We'd head over to the Brighton section, see people leaving the house, wait a long time, then knock at the front door and keep knocking while somebody went around the back and broke a window, getting in. Then he'd let us in the front, as though somebody was home, and then we'd ransack the house, taking everything we could carry.

By fourteen I was shaking down kids in the schoolyard, or the ice cream man, graduating to stick-ups with Pete Russo and Lucky. Hit one army-and-navy store where we locked up an old guy in the bathroom, but all we got out of that was sixty bucks. It didn't take too good getting only sixty for the three of us and it would have been heavy slam time if we were nailed, or we could even have been killed.

Lucky and I nixed going one night, and Pete Russo went on a heist by himself, and he shot a guy dead. He told us afterward at the Winslow Theater that he killed the guy. He was shook up. We all were. You already were schooled enough to know that although you couldn't be implicated in the murder, you could get nailed for the other heists we'd been on. Russo implicated Lucky in the heist, and I lammed, borrowing a guy's name and identification, and just joined the Army.

With hair on my chest, shaving, a big kid at fourteen, I passed as eighteen and was with a cavalry outfit until I hurt my knee five months later. They found out my right age and I was discharged honorably as a minor.

It wasn't long after that Mike the Bandit got his first car, a big '39 La Salle, a big bus, big enough room for ten people. Once he came on the block with Joey alongside, and Joey said, "Hey, Greek, what're you doing?"

"I'm not doing nothing," I said.

"What do you want to do?"

"I don't care."

"Come on, we'll get laid. Get Marilyn."

"Hey," I said. "Yeah."

We drove down Belt Parkway, with Joey and her in the back. Plump, I remember, blonde and blue-eyed, a pretty little bitch giving off with the giggles when Joey was about to throw her a hump. He told us, "Don't be looking now. Don't be looking."

Didn't take him long, and after I climbed in the back with her, it didn't take me long either. Mike wouldn't let any of us drive his car. We had to go all the way to Coney Island, parking under the el by a lot of woods, before he'd plow her, and it was after one in the morning. She was yelling that she had to get home. Joey said maybe she wanted more, and she was saying, "No, no, no. It's late. I'll get killed."

"Then I'll hump you on the way back," Joey said. "That way you won't have anything to yell about."

A couple of times we went horseback riding in Prospect Park. One afternoon we were out on the bridle path, Mike the Bandit wahooing like a goddamned nut, waving his hat around, spooking the horse, and I said to Joey, "What the fuck is he doing?"

"What the fuck is this horse doing?" said Joey.

Mine was listening good, just cantering, but his wasn't listening at all. He got right off, pulling hard on the bridle strap, winding it tight by the bit. The horse tried to jerk its head away, while Joey, cocking a couple of good ones right on the nose, punching that horse silly, yelled, "Listen, you stupid bastard! Listen!"

The horse kept snorting, bobbing its head, like it was trying to shake off what was bothering it. The dumb horse listened after that. That was Joey's way with everybody. If you didn't listen, he'd cock you fast. I guess that horse never ran into anybody like Joey Gallo.

That was pretty much the way it had been when we were kids: hanging out in Blackie's Pool Room or the OK Cafeteria, getting into card games and dice games, block fights between the Irish and the Italians. Standing on the corners with beebop suits, pegged pants and all, or, in the winters, dark coats and white fedoras, doing all that George Raft shit, tossing coins in the air.

Or the time I went to work for Madman Muntz, installing TV aerials, the same work as Blast was doing. Larry worked on the docks then as a longshoreman, and he and Joey wanted Blast to be the smart one and go to college. And I remembered when Larry took over the OK Cafeteria, making it into a nice club called Jackie's. Papa Gallo ran it for a while, then Mama Gallo.

Then there were the Knights of Columbus dances at Prospect Hall, where we got into a hell of a fight one night when Joey punched a guard. A lot of guys sailed into it with tables and chairs, and guys were being thrown down the stairs.

Joey got in with Johnny Bath Beach,* an old-timer who schooled him. Johnny Bath Beach was one bad dude who had at least five to ten notches under his belt, guys that he'd whacked out. That really started the whole thing, and I sort of got into it by just being around.

The hell of it was that in all those years, as fast as Joey could be with his hands and feet, he never once gave me any real shit, and it didn't matter if you were his best friend or not, he'd still nail you if he had a mind to. Only once he gave me mouth, and I walked out on him.

That was after he did that big bit for extortion, and he was having trouble with Jeffie. He called me the next day and said, "Hey, Greek, forget about last night. Was hot with the old lady. Bugs me sometimes. Listen, we've gone through a lot together to—you listening?"

"Yeah, I'm listening."

"I'm trying to apologize, you Greek fuck."

"I know."

"Coming over?"

"Sure."

"Hey, we'll get a couple of broads, maybe something nice like old Marilyn. Whatever happened to her?"

"Don't know. Maybe she got married."

"Well, forget your gummare for tonight, and I'll forget that fucking Jeffie, get some good numbers, go to Greek Town, and have a time, what the fuck."

He could go out of his way, like the time he helped that couple who couldn't have kids and had tried adopting but were forever on a waiting list. They were a nice couple and they wanted a baby real bad. Joey went to all the trouble of finding a girl, some slut who was going to put her baby up for adoption when it was born. He told her how nice the couple was, that they were churchgoers, and that they'd bring up the kid

*John Oddo.

decently and love it, and maybe it wouldn't turn out street people, that she had to think about that. All the selling didn't do it. He had to pay her. Afterward he called her a miserable bitch, saying she had gold between her legs. He wondered if there was a God when a no-good slut could have kids any time she got a good fuck but good people who wanted one so bad couldn't. He really had to shell out for that baby and make it all legal. Those two people will never forget him.

I leaned my hands on his coffin.

"You fuck. You never shed a tear for anybody. Well I'm not shedding a tear for you either. If you only had listened to me, just listened to me, I wouldn't be over your coffin, looking at you, and I'm not going to shed a tear for you.

"You fuck. You had to get all juiced up on the champagne. You had to do that, huh? You had to show them your big balls, huh? You had to go there. Well, I'm shedding no tears, Joey. But I'll tell you one thing. I'll make you this vow. If I can just survive whatever the fuck happens over here, no matter what it is, no matter which way I have to go, somehow, some way, I'll repay who did this to you. I swear that, Joey. I swear that. Hear what I'm telling you?"

I made the sign of the cross and kissed his forehead. But it was hard and cold, and it wasn't any good.

nineteen

In the morning Joey was to be buried. It seemed it would be as it had been with his brother Larry when they closed the coffin. I could only hope that it wouldn't be the same with the family, especially the women, working themselves up with hysterical crying, throwing themselves on the coffin, screaming, "Take me with you!" and *"Why?"* Nobody likes to see that, but it was like that, all screaming and crying, especially his sister Cam. Mama Gallo had to be carried out.

Well, I looked at him for the last time. I stroked his cheek and said a final goodbye. Then they closed the coffin.

After the mass at St. Charles, you saw all the newspaper people and cameras outside; the law too, tagging every car that came, taking pictures of everybody from every angle. They had a panel truck too. They'd be tailing us all the way to the cemetery, even there. Cam, as loud as she could, was still screaming, "Joey, Joey! The streets will run red with blood!"

The line of limousines went slow on President. People were out the windows and along the curbs with their hats off. Then it was on to Greenwich Cemetery, the *benonoma mallari*, the place of the dead.

They were lowering him into his grave, right next to his brother Larry. They weren't only burying Joey. They were burying him and his brother all over again.

But seeing him going down, I asked myself: What did he ever have? He didn't even have enough time on the outside, no time at all.

I looked over at Blast, and anything I ever felt, any respect I ever had, was gone. He never once avenged things in the immediate Family, things that were very personal. How the hell was he going to avenge his brother's death now, his own brother?

Well, I saw Joey going down on the straps. I took a flower and threw it in with him. It was as though I'd thrown something away.

Two days later I bedded down with Blast and Tony Bernardo. We all had gone to the mattresses on President Street.

At Roy-Roy's, Tony Bernardo was by the window when he saw five guys get out of two cars, heading toward Armando's.

"Blast," he called.

Blast put down the *Times,* taking off his glasses, saying, "Who is it now?" When he saw who it was, he said, "Well, let's get over there," then looked around as though he expected ashtrays to be emptied out and everything tidied up. To his back, Tony B made with the middle finger.

At Armando's the five turned out to be Denis Dillon, the head of the Brooklyn strike force, and four of his guys. They had taken one of the tables and had us come up one at a time, after Blast had talked to the lawyer, asking if this was within our constitutional rights, and the lawyer said it was only routine, that it wouldn't hurt, but it would go hard on us if we didn't. So we answered what was asked, which was practically nothing and even silly.

Roll call was heavier with city law, the day shifts, the night shifts, a crew from the homicide division or the DA's office, or else a special crew assigned to organized crime who knew all the faces. Pencil and pad, they'd come in and say, "Hi, Pete. You're here?" I'd say, "I'm here," and they'd check me off. Then they'd go around checking off all the other guys.

Eddy Lambert, who was now retired from the city force, would come around. He wasn't such a big guy, looked Irish, was graying, but he still had law all over him. During the Profaci war he was one hard-nosed cop, and he had a complete file of mug shots and rap sheets on everybody in the back of his car. I think he was the first to make me with the Gallo crew, that I was one of the regulars and not an around guy.

Once he came on me and my old partner, Frankie Rovella, saying that although he couldn't prove it, he knew we'd been into a heist over by Sheepshead Bay. At the same time, he showed us some pictures. You had to see these pictures. They were big and glossy but gruesome, the guy more bones than skin, and he said, "That's your friend."

"What friend?" I said.

"Your friend Ernie the Hawk. Don't you recognize him?"

Well, Lambert knew the Hawk was always in our company, especially when he once busted an afterhours joint and we had been with him. But Ernie the Hawk, from the Genovese crew, was a stoolie, and orders came out from Genovese in jail to clip this guy. He was clipped, all right, and thrown with the fishes, and that's what he looked like when he surfaced, more bones·than skin. Who could recognize that?

Before Joey was killed, when this cop Lambert was semi-retired, he'd mellowed, and he liked to come around and rap with Joey about the Profaci days, like some old soldier talking it out with an old enemy. Joey, who really hated him once, enjoyed rapping with him, and when Lambert did retire, Joey took him to dinner with the Orbachs at an Italian restaurant. I think Eddy Lambert really liked Joey and even some of the crew. He was still pretty sharp and he could read, better than anyone, what our comeoff would be on the Colombos. It was eerie when he made predictions that were right

on, as though he had a wire on us all the time. Then
he'd say, "Don't you know if *I* know, they know too?
Think you fellas ought to think about that." And then
he'd smiled.

For that first week I laid up with Blast at Roy-
Roy's. Blast was waiting for his apartment over Armando's to get finished, having the plumbers and paint-
ers go in and picking out furniture from Cellini's. He
was worse to have around than ten wives. He wouldn't
say it but he expected Tony Bernardo or myself to be
his maid. We weren't about to clean out anybody's
ashtrays.

Most of the time he was reading some book or
other, a regular bookworm, and every morning he'd
read *The New York Times,* saying that was the great-
est paper and the *Daily News* was trash. Well, I could
believe that, all right. The *News* was carrying a story
that the guy who clipped Joey was a loner, some
imported shooter from Sicily. That's how screwed up
they had it.

Blast liked to play chess, calling it therapy of the
mind, and then he'd go into how it had been de-
vised from the medieval days of warfare, as if any of
us were interested. But it taught you how to make
moves, he said.

He was pretty vain, taking off his glasses whenever anyone came in or whenever you talked to him
or looking at his hair in the mirror. He never forgave
Tony Bernardo for telling him to cut it short, that it
would grow in stronger. He cut it short, all right,
and it just stopped growing. He had hair implants put
in that looked like dirty rings until his hair filled in.

That week the Orbachs came down with their
station wagon loaded with Italian food and wine. It
was as though they were the Red Cross and we were
at the front. Well, in a lot of ways we were.

Word came down from Gino, the one from the
Genovese crew, who called my wife. When I called him
back from a safe public phone all the way over on
Atlantic Avenue, I arranged to see him over at Sammy
the Syrian's bar, where he told me he wanted to speak

to Blast about what had happened. A meet was set up
at Papa Gallo's cellar apartment. The word was that
Chin was very concerned that Matty the Horse had had
something to do with Joey's hit. If he had, Gino assured us, Chin would take care of it properly and
promptly.

We discussed the shooting, how it came off, and I
told Gino, "I know Matty was involved. There's no
way I can believe he wasn't. He can't deny to me that
he didn't know the hit was coming off. Why did he
position himself right behind us at the counter, like he
was pointing, where he could be seen from the side
door, then duck into the kitchen just when Pinto came
in? And something else. Pinto did work for him. He
can't go into the guy's place if there's going to be a
comeoff without letting him know. Pinto had to let him
know he was coming in. There's no other way to read it.
Maybe it was the big fat guy with pimples who told
him."

"So why the fuck didn't you shoot Matty?" Gino
asked.

"I had no more bullets in the fucking gun. Other-
wise he wouldn't be here."

"Well, Chin wants to give his condolences," he
said.

He passed an envelope with money to Blast. I just
knew that even if they found out Matty was involved,
they weren't about to take him off. They don't shoot
their big earners, not even when they're ratting out to
the FBI. All that time Gino had been a little jittery even
though we had put the pistols away.

Then Jeffie called from California. She was told
that Blast wasn't around, and when she was asked if
she wanted to speak to anyone else, she said she wanted
to talk to me. She was stoned out of her mind, crying,
saying I was the only one of any of them that she
wanted to talk to, and being killed like that, that was
the way Joey wanted to go. She had wanted to come to
the funeral, but she didn't want to cause problems for
anyone.

"Jeffie, what problems?" I said. "You deserved
being there more than anybody."

She still loved him, and I told her I knew Joey still loved her even after the divorce, but I didn't tell her that it was Joey's way of paying her back for having married that English guy or the guys he thought she might have been with when he'd been in the slams.

Well, I felt bad for her, and I wanted Blast to make his moves, not chess moves but hard moves on the Colombos, and if Sonny Pinto ever surfaced we'd both go on him, and I would have the pleasure of going first. That was the only thing working on me, to clip that sonofabitch. I tried every way I knew to get a line on where he'd gone. But I came up empty.

twenty

Now we were getting ready to attack the Colombos. First we had to learn where the opposition was located, what patterns they were making. From information being fed back to us, we learned they hadn't gone to the mattresses, but they'd tightened up. If they moved at all, it was never predictable, and never with their own cars, so you couldn't make them easily. They either hired a limousine service or rental cars with "Z" plates that were switched every week.

We had a special tab for Nicky Bianco, but he'd lammed to Providence. But our main targets were those who would be moving for the Colombo throne, or who might already be on it, like the two capos Vinnie Aloi and Charley Moose,* and at one point I'd heard Charley Moose was already on the throne. Sammy the Syrian was to go for Vinnie Aloi, and I was to go for Charley Moose.

We found out that the Moose had an afterhours club, a fag joint over on Fourteenth Street between

*Charles Panarella.

170

Second and Third in Manhattan. Castro, a Puerto Rican, the newcomer in the Mod Squad, had never done a piece of heavy work, and Blast told me to take him along, to see what was with the guy, if he really had it in him. So for a couple of nights we worked surveillance. Castro didn't have it in him.

We were parked beautifully to tag the Moose, but that last night, even though it was April, it was cold, and we'd been parked for about an hour and a half when Castro started moaning, "How long are we going to stay here?"

"As long as it takes," I said.

Then he started bitching about the cold and how he had a date, and he kept on bitching for the next two hours. What did this guy think it was—like the movies, where the tag comes off so easy in no time at all? Those Colombos aren't stupid. You got to do a lot of maneuvering. You got to wait and wait and clock a guy right. No target is going to sit still for you. That's only in the fucking movies.

Well, I had it with that guy telling me how he had to see some barmaid he was going with, when here we were out to do a piece of work. It was morning but it was still dark when I left Castro off, telling him, "Go to your fucking broad, just go."

Back at the apartment, Blast was asleep. I got him up, all right, and even he was complaining that he hadn't had his coffee yet when I told him, "Listen, Blast, this bullshit of sending me with a new guy who's a constant complainer, who just wants to be with his fucking broad, and he keeps bellyaching, I don't go for. It turns me right off. So don't send him, don't put him with me again. I want no part of a bullshit guy."

"Okay," he said. Then he said, "Wait till we hear from Sammy."

Sammy the Syrian had told us that there was a big driveway out front of Vinnie Aloi's house, with lots of bushes, beautiful for laying to take him off. That was where he'd gone that morning. When Sammy got back that afternoon, he said it was a no show. Blast went into how important these two Colombos were. We had to take them off. It was a must. Once we had, we would be in a better bargaining position. Then he said the three were the most important. And I said, "What three?"

"Include Allie Boy," he said.

Joe Yak, the consigliere, had the big say-so. He'd be the most important, and I'd laid for him over on Seventh Avenue, and it was a no show. But Junior's brother Allie Boy Persico, that was something else again, as far as Blast was concerned.

Both Junior and Apples McIntosh had been sent away to do big federal time about a month before, and right about then Allie Boy had been made a good fellow by the Erie, Pennsylvania, boss, Russ Bufalino. It was supposed to have been done quietly, but what was amazing was that it was so quiet, it was in the newspapers a week later.

That more than perturbed Blast, who obviously envied Allie Boy and wanted him taken off. He wanted him so bad that it was one of the rare times Blast ever came down from the bleachers to try for the heavy work.

Sammy and Louie had a line through a connection and were to go on Allie Boy at a café over on Fifth Avenue, clock him right, then hit him. But the morning that Blast went out, he took me and Smokey the Bear,* another of the regulars, but a guy nobody trusted. Smokey had already gotten into the panel truck, and I was coming around, when I noticed that I could see him through the window. I thought maybe it was the sun, that you could see into the one-way glass when the sun was right on it, just as you could with a one-way mirror when lights were behind it. But when I went around to all the windows, I could see clear inside.

I grabbed Blast and I said, "Thought these windows were supposed to be one-way."

"Well, they wanted three hundred and fifty dollars. So I had them tinted instead."

I looked at him. I didn't say a word. I thought back to the time we were laying heavy surveillance on

*Joseph D'Antuano.

Joe Colombo and the time Apples McIntosh had been out on the porch of Colombo's funeral parlor, when the kid tried the door handles, then tried to look inside. And here was Blast—who you knew, if ever a fall came, would never be implicated, would never be around to get implicated—risking our lives so he could save a dime.

Over at Dolly's a few days later Blast told me we were setting out to go on Allie Boy again. Then he said, "I'm getting Bobby D to participate in it."

He knew I wasn't talking to Darrow, that whenever he came into Dolly's or Armando's, I would walk out. Blast said, "So try not to show any friction between yourselves. It's not good for the men."

"Listen," I said, "I can't take to the guy anymore. With everything that happened to Joey, I just can't."

"Well, okay. Let's talk about it some other time. I see that particular topic gets you a little irritated."

"A little?"

"All right, but try to keep your differences from the men, especially for the next couple of days."

"When do we move?"

"When it's right," he said.

Allie Boy lived near Bath Avenue, close to Shore Parkway, in a one-family house, separated by shrubs and hedges from the next house, only twenty feet away.

Bobby Darrow was to team up with Preston,* a kid in the Mod Squad, an unpredictable kid so ballsy he was crazy. Joey had the right name for him. The Nut. Some shooting team they'd make.

One night the surveillance team reported that there was a lot of activity at Allie Boy's, that Jerry Lang, Andy Mush, and three other Colombos had been seen going in and were still inside, probably in the finished basement, since all the lights were on. Blast liked that.

That made six Colombo shooters, not counting whoever else was inside. With Darrow and Preston we only had two. Bobby Boriello would be at the wheel of the lead car, while Roy-Roy and I would be in the

*Preston Geritano.

backup. But we would be a block away. It would be suicide. In fact, that was what Blast was calling them, the Suicide Squad, and high bleacher that he was, he wasn't going, especially on this one.

At Dolly's he'd already talked to Darrow and Preston at their table, and he was grinning.

"All right," Blast said to us.

I asked, "Those two idiots know there are six guys inside, maybe more?"

"They know."

"Well, let's go and do it. It's their asses on the fire."

"Wait. I think you guys ought to wait a while."

"Wait for what?"

"Roll call. It's about that time," he said.

Not long after that two detectives from homicide came in, one going around to the tables with his pad and pencil, the other having a cup of coffee, talking to Blast. At our table we were playing gin rummy, and the one with the pad asked how we were doing. "Lousy," I said. I had Roy-Roy beat a mile.

He went off with Blast over to Armando's, while the other kept on with his coffee. Then he had another one with a bun, even though it was probably stale by now. He was the sort that would get nervous if you talked to him, so I talked to him, saying, "Hey, how about a little anisette in your coffee?"

He said nothing.

"Well, how about playing a hand with us?" I asked.

"Would that look right, Pete? That wouldn't look right."

"Yeah, you're right," I said. "It wouldn't."

He went out then without saying anything, still chewing on his bun, just looking around before he did. Jimmy Springs checked him going into Armando's. Blast was really making it good for himself. He was sure to keep them around for a while and even bring them up to his apartment. Roy-Roy said he'd probably have them tuck him in afterward.

"Let's do what we have to," I told him. I wouldn't

tell the other guys. I had him tell them. Then we all ducked out the back, going for the two cars.

The street in back of Allie Boy's was quiet. It was a clear night, the big moon lighting up everything. Then, when the moon went behind a cloud, it would go dark again. That was when Bobby Darrow and Preston got out of the lead car, holding the pump shotguns along their legs before going between the two houses for the yard. All the while Roy-Roy and I watched them from the backup.

Then the moon came out again, lighting everything like gray-silver almost. But you couldn't see them with all the dark trees. Then a light came on from the back of one of the houses, and you could see them in the yard, all right, crawling on their elbows and knees, the shotguns cradled in their arms. The two went flat, not moving. They just lay there. Then you saw Darrow crawling ahead. Preston followed, going faster, the soles of his shoes and his rump all wiggly till he made the dark.

"Think anybody saw them?" asked Roy-Roy.

"How do I know?"

"But anybody could have seen them."

"Hey, nobody's looking like we're looking," I said.

If anybody had spotted them, we'd find sector cars all over, and Roy-Roy had to keep reminding me of that. He said maybe it was best if I got them out of there. I told him, "Too late now. We can't back out."

I tried to pacify him. He was the kind of guy you had to pacify a lot, a moody guy, ballsy only if it was in front of him. But to go out and do a piece of work, he wouldn't do it, and he was sort of lazy. You had to present it to him on a platter.

Joey called him Mama's Boy whenever Roy-Roy started with the complaints. "What a fucking ball-buster," Joey would say. "Hey, go home to your mama, stay there, don't leave, and don't come back till I tell you to come back."

Well, there I was thinking about Joey when I had to concern myself with the work.

I couldn't make Allie Boy's house too well, except for the one upstairs light and the lights from the basement. Darrow and Preston had to be there by now. You couldn't hear much, except for a dog barking. Sometimes a car went by, but that was all. We waited for those explosions. I was going tight. I lowered the window, laying the shotgun on my lap.

Just then a couple came out of the house behind us. The guy had his keys out, the woman trailing with her arms folded and her shoulders hunched. The guy was bawling her out, saying, "Why don't you just move in with your stupid mother and be done with it?"

She told him, "Keep your big trap shut. You'll wake up the whole neighborhood."

He didn't stop yelling.

As they left in their car, I saw something between the two houses. It was Bobby Darrow coming over to us.

"Greek," he said, "we've got them good."

"How good?"

"Real good. They're all in the cellar."

"So do what you got to do. What're you coming back here for?"

"Blast said to cool it if there was a broad in there like his old lady. She's there, and the kid's upstairs. We don't have to know there was a broad and a kid there."

Just then I thought about Joey again. I had to get to that. I asked Darrow, "They think about Joey with his wife and the kid?"

"We'll take them good."

"Wait a fucking minute. I have to think about this. Where's Preston?"

"Still laying there."

"Tell you what. See if they're coming out. Grab them then."

"Greek, we can always say we didn't see the broad and the kid."

"Think we'd better cool it," said Roy-Roy.

"Yeah," I said. I was sure that Darrow would go back and blow the place apart.

"But we can get them all good," said Darrow.

"Yeah, real good," I said. "But I know what Blast

would say. 'Let's pass.' We're passing. Cool it. Now get Preston."

"Ah, for Christ's sake."

"I told you, we're passing."

"This was all for nothing," Darrow said, then he headed away.

Roy-Roy said, "Pete, you did the right thing. I'm glad of that."

"Well, I'm not," I said.

A couple of days later Darrow wanted to go back to Allie Boy's. That Blast was considering it meant Darrow was crazy enough to do anything. It would be right if we caught Allie Boy outside the house, but catching him in the house with the wife and the kid, that wouldn't go down so good.

I was still avoiding Darrow. The one time I'd talked to him at all was that night at Allie Boy's and only because I had to. Blast didn't like that at all. So one evening at Armando's, Sammy the Syrian came around the tables, and over to mine. "Blast wants to see you," he said.

I picked up my coffee, taking it with me. Upstairs, in the kitchen, they were all around the table— Blast, Punchy, Louie the Syrian, and Bobby Darrow. They were all in their shirtsleeves. Sammy came around me, taking a chair. Blast said, "Sit down, Pete. Finish your coffee. Have a cigarette."

I said nothing.

"Well," said Blast, "we're all here because we want to straighten out the differences you have with Bobby."

"Listen, I have no differences. I just don't want to be bothered with the guy."

You could see Darrow going jittery and tight.

"Yeah," I said. "Yeah. I don't want to be bothered, and nobody in the world, not even Al Capone or Jesus Christ, can make me talk to this guy."

Blast came over the table, grabbing me by the chin, squeezing hard, yelling, "Listen, I'm telling you!"

"Hey, Blast, I'm not talking to the guy. I've got my reasons."

"What's your reasons? Tell us your reasons!"

"My reasons are he's a weak individual. Period. I just can't take to the guy anymore."

Darrow came off his chair, his eyes dancing, the way he'd go when he wanted to shoot somebody. "Whatta you mean weak? Whatta you mean by that fucking weak?"

"Sit down!" yelled Blast. Then to me, "All right. Now, Greek, tell us what you mean."

"Yeah," said Darrow, "I want to hear."

"You want to hear?" I said. "You're a fucking pill head, a pot head, a fucking snorter. You're out of control. It controls you. And I just don't want to be around a guy like you. I just don't want to be bothered. Now if there's nothing else, I'm getting up and I'm leaving."

"Sit down there," said Blast.

"Blast, what's there to sit down about?"

"I'm telling you to sit down."

"Yeah, I'm sitting down. Now what? Now what do you want to talk about?"

"You're a fucking thick-headed Greek, that's all it is with you."

"That's what I am, Blast. But if you don't mind, I'm leaving," I said.

Over at Roy-Roy's apartment I packed my bag and had Castro drive me home, staying three days with my own family.

twenty-one

I don't think Bobby Darrow was any different when I first met him in the early sixties, just as crazy, but controllable at least. He was tied in with two street guys named Sonny and Dino, and they were all getting a piece of a bar, which was affiliated with a Times Square hotel. An hour before closing, the registers and tapes would stop, and whatever came in after that was theirs.

The Profaci war was on. We were low on bread and I'd gone to Larry Gallo, looking to make a move on the bar. Larry said to check it out. Through a friend of mine I got in as a weekend bartender. The information I was getting was that everybody was robbing everybody.

Darrow and the other two street guys were leery of me, making me for a different kind of guy, that I was working for the one partner to spy on them. One day Porky, a knock-around guy I knew from Mulberry Street, came in asking what I was doing there, and I told him I was looking to earn, to hook up with the joint. He said, "You crazy? It's connected already. It's

179

Sally Burns'."* Sally was a made guy, a good fellow from the Genovese crew. There was no sense hanging around. But Porky had introduced me to Bobby Darrow and the other two guys, and I sort of got tight with Darrow after that.

It wasn't more than three weeks later that he went to jail. He'd gotten loaded on VO, going over like the Tower of Pisa, with that funny hop when he walked, and I'd told him to go up to his hotel room and sleep it off, but he wanted to go home to his wife and kid. Well, he got home, all right, only the wife wasn't there. The babysitter was. He screwed her and she yelled rape. The law hit him for that one and violation of parole for robbery, sending him to Attica. I didn't see him again for two years.

Sonny was supposed to stake him when he came out, and maybe he'd given him some bucks. But Bobby ran up such a tab at his hotel that they locked him out of his room, putting the pin in his lock. Sonny, who we both knew, had made a big twenty-grand score with Mike, Sally Burns' kid. He told Darrow he didn't have the bread. Darrow saw his colors, realized that Sonny was just using him, and he came in with me. After that Darrow and I were inseparable.

He had good balls, knew the streets, was prison wise, and I brought him into the crew. He still was a long way from knowing how to maneuver, how to do things right, how not to leave doors open so the law could make us. And he had to be the clumsiest guy I ever knew. He was just big thumbs loading a pistol, and he had to be the worst shot in the world, besides being the world's worst driver. Twice I had to jump out of the car he was driving. He'd wrecked a couple, and he'd tell me afterward that he was really getting good, that he could really handle a wheel now, and that he was getting better with the pistol besides. I guess the way he thought he was getting good was to shoot somebody, like he shot Apples McIntosh that time.

Together we did a lot of things. We were moving good after I schooled him on working paper scores,

*Salvatore Granello.

how to handle paper right. We moved a lot of paper. We worked marks, giveups, and hijacks, pulled stick-ups with no comebacks, worked good burglaries, and had shylock money on the street.

We moved around a lot of Manhattan bars and clubs, hooked up with plenty. One was by the old Madison Square Garden, where we got in working as managers and bouncers. One night when the owner was going through the register, bagging the cash, I told him he needed a new partner, and when he answered, "Don't be silly," I said, "I don't think so," pulling the pistol. Then I told him to get on his knees and open his mouth. Then I stuck the barrel in his mouth and told him, "Since I'm your new partner, it's only fair that we share equally on the register." And that was the start of that club. Then we opened the after-hours club upstairs, which was no problem, as the hotel owner never asked for the rent, and for eight months or more we only paid him for two months.

The afterhours thing didn't go off that well, so we tried Chinese food and that wasn't any better. Then we turned the club into a fag joint. It was jammed every night after that with all sorts of gay guys and transvestites who'd had the operations, the female hor-mone injections, and damned if they didn't look like women, some of them even beautiful.

Gays would come over and ask us to dance. We'd say we were straight and let it go at that, and I told Bobby Darrow not to hassle them or bust them, that he'd destroy the place, and he said not to worry, that he would treat them as poor unfortunates. After all, it was money. I said, "That's right, and that's all we should concern ourselves with."

Well, one night when it was packed as usual, a tittery sort of gay came over to our table, asking us to dance, working her mouth like it was set up with alum. We told her we were straight guys. About fifteen min-utes later she came again, and I said to her, "You were just over here. I told you. We're straight guys."

Before going to the kitchen, I told Darrow, who was getting sauced, to be nice, even if it killed him. Well, from the kitchen I heard screaming and glasses breaking, tables and chairs screeching, and more clatter. There was Bobby Darrow pinning the same gay to the floor with his knees and punching hell out of her. I pulled Bobby right off, and she began swinging at him, trying to kick from the floor, while Bobby wanted to come out with the slapper—that's flatter than a blackjack but can do a lot of damage. I pinned his arms, getting him back to the table, while all the gays were screaming.

My front guy, the manager, looked really worried, saying that was the queen bee, and I said, "Holy shit." The queen bee came charging at our table, holding her head back, still trying to slap Bobby Darrow. I held my arm out, stopping her, saying, "Just wait a moment, please. I'm in charge here." Then I whispered to Darrow, "You stupid fuck. That's the queen bee. Apologize to her."

Darrow, realizing what he had done, was lame about it but apologized. She screamed that he was an animal, a terrible animal, and that she would never come here ever again, and neither would her friends ever come here again, never, ever. I was saying, "If you'll just calm down," while Bobby, with all the mouthing she was giving him, wanted to go on her again. She kept screaming he was an animal. We all were animals.

Well, where the queen bee goes, the gays follow. She never came back and neither did anyone else. It was finished after that. Bobby Darrow really did a job on that club. He destroyed it.

Another bar we moved on, we'd hooked up good. But one night Red Lebowitz, a bad dude in his time, all dappered up in a black raincoat, came over to me at the bar. He said, "You Pete?"

"Yeah, I'm Pete."

"I'm your new partner."

"Don't quite understand you."

"I said I'm your new partner."

"Still don't quite understand you. Let's go in the back and have a drink. Maybe this way we can clear up what you're trying to tell me."

"Yeah. Why not?"

At a table, I sat across from him. The tables were loaded, the floor crowded with dancers. The band was going. Red still sat with his raincoat on.

I said, "You mind going over what you just said, what you're indicating, that you're *my* new partner?"

"Yeah."

"Well, I don't think you're functioning properly, I think there's something wrong."

Red leaned over the table. "Nothing's wrong. And furthermore I don't give a fuck who you're with."

I grabbed the lapels of his raincoat, pulling him over the table, hooking him a good one, knocking him into people dancing. Then I was all over him on the floor, had him by the throat, taking the life out of him, when Bobby Darrow and three guys pulled me away.

Darrow didn't know what was happening, and while the three guys held onto me, Darrow asked Red, "What's happening over here?"

Red said, "Tell your partner, whoever he is, I'm coming back for him."

"You're what?" Darrow said, and hit him across the mouth with the slapper, wrecking all his front teeth, then dumped him in the garbage can outside, kicking it, rolling it down the street with Red in it.

I was getting tired of bars. But all Darrow wanted was to have his own place, not just being hooked up and getting the percentage, so he opened up a club in Brooklyn. I passed on that and went on my own with the barboot game in Greek Town, where nobody had ever ran the barboot game before.

You can whack a lot out of barboot, a fast dice game, none faster, but you had to whack a lot back every month. Five hundred went to the detectives, three hundred to the sergeants, a big twelve hundred to Borough and Division, and another hundred-and-fifty to sector cars. This wasn't counting my overhead or all my people, or laying a grand on Joe Colombo as a present from Blast, and Colombo expecting it every month. Everybody was into it. But the law got more than Joe Colombo. So I guess that cop, Serpico, had a real beef.

But it hadn't been so easy getting the game started when guys like Tony Boots, Dolls, and Bybee came on me. Dolls and Bybee, two Gambinos, were with O'Neil,* while Tony Boots, a good fellow, was with the Harlem crew. It seemed I was infringing on their barboot blocks away, and Tony Boots started with the bullshit about guys who'd tried it who'd been taken off, or just had their legs broken. Well, I'd put my balls in that game and nobody was chasing me. I went on him, chasing him right out of Greek Town.

That was a big beef since Boots was a good fellow, something you're not supposed to do, and it had to go for the sitdown with Joe Colombo and Mr. Gribbs, the Harlem boss. Since Joe Colombo got his grand, and Blast even had me buy him a diamond watch and another time a golf cart (and all we ever got back from Joe C was cheap ties for Christmas), I kept my game.

Well, Tony Boots wasn't finished. He sent the law down on me, the same law I had on the pad, so the Greeks would see that I didn't have the good protection like they had. But I had the right shmeer, and I re-opened again the following night and stayed open, and didn't close the game until I wanted it closed. That was one of the few things I didn't partner with Darrow.

One time Darrow came to me, saying this guy from Jersey, loaded with bread, wanted somebody taken off. The first thing I asked was if he saw the guy, or talked to him. When he said no, that he had the particulars from the guy's nephew through another guy and had a number to call, I said, "Good." Then I told him how we were going to maneuver it.

I called the guy. "Ronald?" I said.

"Yes."

"I understand you have a problem, and you're looking for somebody to take care of the problem."

He was hesitant. "Who is this?"

"Better for you and me that you don't know. But we were put onto it by your nephew Bill. Bill spoke to some mutual friends. Understood?"

*Aniello Dellacroce, the underboss.

"Yes, I understand."

"Now, here's what I want you to do. Go to a public phone, get the number, and I'll call you back. Is there one by your house?"

"Yes, a block or so."

"Fine. I'll call you back in fifteen minutes."

After we did all that, and I got him to the outside phone, I asked, "Now, Ronald, what seems to be your problem?"

"In specific terms?"

"Not too specific."

"Well, it has to do with a final termination. Do you understand my meaning?"

"Of course. But that's a very steep thing you're talking about."

"Well, I'd like to meet you and discuss it, and perhaps you can terminate this matter for me."

"I'm not in that particular business, but I can get you set up with some people who will assist you. Be at this phone in one hour."

"What if some people want to use this phone?"

"You just wait, Ronald," I said.

We were the somebody, and I had Darrow make the appointment at a room at the Waldorf. Before Ronald ever came into the hotel, we put on fifty-dollar suits and took off the jewelry. I cut up a pair of my wife's stockings, put them on us, then left only one lamp lit. The knock came on the door and he said who he was. He was really rattled when he saw the stockinged face coming out from behind the door. I said, "Hello, Ronald."

"Yes," he said.

"Sit down, Ronald. No sense knowing my name, is there? Just call me Number One."

Just then Darrow came out of the bathroom with the stocking pulled down. I said, "Ronald, this here's my associate, Number Two."

"Mr. One and Mr. Two," he said. "All right."

"Now," I said, "what's this you're looking to do?"

"Can we speak openly?"

"Yes."

"Well, I want my wife killed."

"You want your wife killed. Very good. But it takes quite a bit of money to take care of something like that. Are you in the position to pay?"

"Yes, I am."

"Well, we can do a nice job of it."

"That's what I want. You two gentlemen, Mr. One and Mr. Two, seem quite capable."

"We are. It will cost you five thousand for the work, and a thousand dollars for expenses."

He agreed on it.

"All right," I said. "Here's the particulars we'll need. A picture of your wife, picture of your house, where it's located. Want the keys to your house, and when she's home and when you leave."

"Ideally it will be when I'm out of town at a convention in Chicago. But that will be in one week. Will that be a problem for you?"

"Shouldn't," I said, and then told him, "Meet us in two days. Bring a thousand, the pictures, and all the particulars. We want everything."

"Fine. Then it's arranged?"

"It's arranged," I said.

Two days later we met him, the same way, Mr. One and Mr. Two. He brought the money, the keys, and the pictures. His wife was a beautiful woman.

He said, "I'd like to explain the reasons why I want this done."

"Don't want to know your reasons," I said. "Your reasons are your own."

We laid on the guy's block in Jersey, had his wife clocked, had everything figured, including his dog, which he hadn't told us about. When he met us again at the Hotel Taft, before going to Chicago, he brought the five thousand. He was built pretty good, broad shoulders, a little bald, in his late thirties, and he spoke very well, but I didn't like it when he said the only problem was his daughter was going to be home with her, his nine-year-old daughter. I thought to myself, the lousy sonofabitch.

We were going to burn him for the six thou, burglarize his place (probably had a wall safe with stocks and bonds, not to mention Treasury notes and cash), then blackmail him besides. But we let too much time pass.

One night Darrow and I were both sauced, and I asked, "What about Ronald?" He said, "Yeah, let's work him," and I said, "Why not?"

So I called him. "Hello, Ronald."

"Yes?"

"This is Mr. One and Mr. Two."

"Oh, how *are* you? Thanks a lot. You're really a fine bunch of guys."

"Well, what we're going to do now is reveal everything to your wife."

"Oh, really? Well, why don't you tell her now? She's right here."

I hung up. If he was that crazy to have his wife murdered with a kid in the house, he was crazy enough to have told her that he'd paid somebody to have her taken off. Well, at least we got six grand out of that one.

Another time Blast called us in, telling us about this guy Stan who was involved in an extortion on a Chinaman, and Mooney was sure that Stan was going to open up on the shylock he and Mooney had been involved with. "Well," said Blast, "we're going to have to dig a hole for this guy." Then he asked me where we could put this guy away, and I said I knew a place upstate, near Fishkill. "Well, start digging the hole," said Blast, and I asked, "How big is this guy?" He looked at both of us and said, "About the same size as Bobby."

We went upstate and dug the hole. It was summer and it was hot. No one made us from the dirt road. The bugs were eating us. We were taking turns, and Darrow was sweating, slapping at his neck in the hole. We were down about three feet when I said to Darrow, "This guy, Stan, he's as big as you. Lay down. Try it. See how it's shaping up."

He stopped shoveling. "What?"

"See if it fits."

He threw out the shovel, took the pick behind him, holding onto it for a while, then threw that, all the time watching me.

"Go 'head," I said. "We have to have the right hole for the guy."

So he lay down. I stood looking at him, grinning. "You're laying there like it's for you."

He got right up. He was jittery, all right. "Whatta you mean by that?"

"Come on," I said. "Start digging. We still have another foot to go."

All the while he shoveled he kept watching me, then the road. You felt that he was wondering not so much if anyone was out there but if anyone was laying for him. Then he just shrugged and kept digging.

Another time when he'd hurt his leg in a beef, he stayed over at his sister's out near Garrison Beach in Brooklyn, and he called me late one night, saying, "Come right over to my sister's. I've got to talk to you."

"You want me to come over to your sister's now?"

"It's a good thing, a very good thing."

I wondered how good it was. Anything he ever came up with, except for Ronald, was usually zero. But I said, "All right. I'll be over in an hour."

It turned out that his brother-in-law was telling him about this *Screw* magazine that he worked for, and that the owner, some guy named Goldstein, wasn't so happy with his distributor, felt he wasn't getting a fair shake, and wanted to know if we could be instrumental in helping Goldstein get the distribution away from them. Darrow said we could work it that he knew all the truck routes, and I said, "Yeah? How in the fuck did you ever drive a truck for *The New York Times?* You can't even drive a car, never mind a truck. I still don't believe you worked for the *Times,* or you must've bullshitted them you could drive a truck."

"Come on, will you. The important thing is I know all the newsstands, all the magazine and paper routes in Manhattan practically."

"Yeah, that would be the important thing," I said.

If we took over the distributorship, set it all up for ourselves, we could all knock up something pretty good and really earn. Darrow said we could start it, then let his sister and brother-in-law work it. We'd put in maybe a week's work setting it up, then get the right percentage after that from his sister and brother-in-law.

Darrow had his brother-in-law call Al Goldstein to make an appointment for us. Monday or Tuesday of that week we drove over to this broken-down building in Greenwich Village. In a messed-up office we saw this Al Goldstein, a real beatnik, going into all the problems he was having with his distributor, wanting to know if we could straighten them out. I told him it wouldn't be any trouble, but we'd have the distributorship, although he'd be getting a better shake, that he'd do a lot better. He was convinced and happy, and he asked if I was acquainted with his magazine. Darrow, smiling, said he was, while I said, "Can't say as I am." Well, this Goldstein handed me his magazine. It had to be the filthiest magazine I'd seen in my entire life.

Afterward, when I was heading back with Darrow, I said, "Tell me something. What in the *fuck* are we getting involved with over here?"

"Whatsamatter? You got principles?"

"That's the worst shit."

"So what's so different between this and the fag joint?"

"Well, I didn't see them blowing anybody," I said.

We must have been the first wiseguys who ever worked it in the open. Some crews were secretive about it, saying they wouldn't be associated with such shit, that it was real garbage, but at the same time seeing big money in it, and the bigger the money became, the more they came out in the open. Now a lot of crews are out in the open, with films, dildos, every aspect of porno, turning it into a bigger business than it ever was.

Well, after we talked to Goldstein, we went on the three guys who had the distributorship, just telling them what they could expect if they didn't cooperate nicely and forgo their agreement with Goldstein. The three guys were shook, but one came out saying they were hooked up with Vince, and I said, "What Vince?" He said I'd know, the boss, the guy they call Chin, over on Sullivan Street. I told him we'd get right back to them, and that he'd better be right about that.

Chin didn't know anything about it, and he was also angry, saying, "I'm going to send for this guy. He just mentions that I know anything about it, I'm going to break his fucking head, because he's a liar. What's he going to do, give me a piece now, after he didn't have this on record for four years, and he's been taking in all the greens for himself, and now he's looking for a rabbi to bail him out of the troubles he's in? No. Whatever it is, it's yours. We don't want no part of it."

That's all we needed. We caught up to one of the distributor's trucks on Ninth Avenue, chased the driver, then busted out the windshield, fucking up the tires. The distributor was now convinced that this was going to happen to all his trucks, and he had no trouble putting it in writing that the contract no longer existed between him and Goldstein.

Every morning for about three weeks we set out with a panel truck, distributing that magazine to all the newsstands. We only had the route started and we were pulling in over eight hundred a week. It was going very good and it would get better.

Then Darrow's sister and brother-in-law made themselves partners, buying a truck and figuring us in for a percentage. But once Blast saw that something like that could get very lucrative, he moved right in, saying the percentage wasn't good enough and pushing Darrow's sister and brother-in-law out of it. She threatened to go to the DA, and Blast said that wouldn't be very sensible. She and her husband were out of it.

Then Blast pushed us out, letting Ricky DiMatteo, one of our regulars, and his gummare work it. Well, Darrow was more than just disturbed about the whole thing, while I was no longer interested in it. It had gotten too out of hand, first with Darrow's family, then with Blast. Darrow was hurting. Many times he brought it up, and I told him, "Listen, you got any beefs? You tell Blast, because you're right."

So he sat down with Blast. But all Darrow really knew was standup and the streets, and he could never express himself properly. Blast made him wrong. Darrow was a hundred percent right, but Blast made him all wrong. Afterward, when I had Blast alone, I told him, "You didn't do the right thing, and you know you didn't. It's very disappointing for me to have to listen to this. As for me, I'm not even interested anymore, but for my partner, and he's hurting, I am interested. It just wasn't right and you know it. And, Blast, I don't even want to talk to you about it anymore."

All he did was smile. Well, I guess he envisioned going national with distribution, because he kept talking about it, that it wasn't only papers and magazines but book publishers and everything else, and he was looking into all the distributors, wanting to make moves on them.

The *Daily Mirror* had long gone under, then it was coming out again as the *Mirror*. Blast had already negotiated the distributorship and now was looking to set up financing for all the trucks we would need. Then Joe Colombo saw what the comeoff would be, and he got into it. Colombo came up with financing the trucks, taking over the distributorship, cutting us out of it. Blast was foaming at the mouth. Now he knew how Darrow felt. It had been the bigger fish eating the little fish, then the biggest, Joe Colombo, eating it all.

Well, Darrow and I had been through a lot, I suppose, and that wasn't nearly all of it. Darrow was a standup guy who would do anything for you, and that meant anything, as loyal a guy as you could possibly find. But when the pressure was on, you found he wasn't really built for it, that even before Joey came home and moved on Colombo, Darrow was going heavier on booze, along with popping pills, blowing pot and hash, and snorting coke. Then when he came into the hospital stoned after I'd been shot and later went to Greek Town to shake down friends of mine, saying the thousand was for me but really blowing it on himself buying four suits—it was like he'd turned out Joey's pockets after they'd killed him.

twenty-two

Weeks after Joey's killing, a story in *The New York Times* by Nick Gage named Joey's killers, and reported that one of them, Joe Pesh, had gone to the feds and had opened up. The way the sonofabitch told it, I was able to put together other things. He had been at Umberto's that night, having a bowl of red chowder, talking to Matty the Horse, when they heard a commotion outside—some guy called Johnny the Iceman was arguing with a cop—and then he'd made us in the Caddy when I pulled up.

He claimed he'd turned away fast so I wouldn't make him as a guy doing work for Joe Yak, the Colombo consigliere, and that he'd made Joey and me with a lot of broads, but he didn't know that it was his wife and sister and hadn't seen the kid.

Well, first of all, this Pesh, who can't read or write, an illiterate, I'd made as a gofer, a nothing guy, hooked up to petty shit, and no Colombo, and if he'd turned away as fast as he claimed, I would have definitely known something was wrong, not just gotten bad feelings about the place.

Another thing, I'd driven around the block, so he couldn't have been all that sure that we had gone into Umberto's unless he'd seen us park and go in, and he had to have seen the kid, Lisa. And even if the sonofabitch couldn't read, he must have known about the wedding just three weeks before, when that picture of Joey with Sina cutting the wedding cake was in all the papers. That sonofabitch had to know that it was Joey's wife.

But he went into how he had gone straight over to the café on 91 Mulberry Street and told Sonny Pinto, Fat Fungi,* and the two brothers, Benny and Cisco, that we were there at Umberto's. Then how Pinto called Joe Yak, telling him Joey was at Umberto's, and Yak was to have said, "What're you waiting for?" Then how they loaded up.

Joe Pesh and Fat Fungi were to stay with the car, to block off Hester and Mulberry, while Pinto and the two brothers, Benny and Cisco, were to do the work. He described how Pinto went through the side door, followed by the brothers, and he'd heard shots right away, and while Pesh was out in the car, where he couldn't have seen anything, he said I ducked under the table, when I wasn't supposed to, and got shot in the ass. And the order, or the bullshit, the way he gave it, was that the next thing I did was stick the pistol to Matty's head. He claimed I kept pulling the trigger, hitting off empty, and every time I pulled it, Matty's head would jerk, and that he could see all this from the open front door, that he could see right into the kitchen.

Then how Joey came out the front door, stumbling and falling right in the middle of Hester Street, with Joey's sister Cam, Sina, and her kid screaming over him. Then I ran out to Joey, and according to Pesh I fainted right there.

Then after Pinto and the two brothers piled in the car, they went back to the café, only about a block or so away. Pinto wanted to keep drinking. Pesh said they had to get out of there. The brothers were given the pistols, to dump them.

*Philip Gambino, no relation to Carlo.

The two, Benny and Cisco, were dropped off at Centre and Grand, right by a precinct house. Then they drove over to where Sonny Pinto had his own car, on Lafayette between Broome and Grand, since Pesh's car had a flat. I had hit their tire, all right.

He told how they drove up to Nyack, with Sonny laying down in the back seat, and when they got to a riverside apartment, they were all excited telling Joe Yak about it. Yak kissed Pinto on the mouth, saying all along he knew he would kill the sonofabitch. Then he asked who else was there, and when he was told that it was Matty, people, some broads, and the Greek, Yak said, "Pete the Greek? Is he dead?"

Pinto didn't know. They shot me and I went to the floor. Yak was worried that I still was alive. The broads were no problem, they didn't know the faces, but I could make all of them.

They listened to a news broadcast saying that Joey had been shot, but nothing else. It really worried Yak that Joey could still be alive. He kept walking up and down and asked what car they used, and when Pesh said he used his, Pinto his, Yak must have felt like going through the floor and must have cursed them for being so stupid, saying they really cowboyed it. Then he asked where Pesh's car was now. He was told it was in front of Pinto's mother's house, that it had a flat, that it had a bullet in it. Yak really must have started cursing. He told them they'd have to go back and get it, change the tire, and take it over to John's place and have it smashed.

Then came the news bulletin on the radio. Joey was dead. They all kissed Sonny Pinto on the mouth.

After laying up in Nyack, Pesh must have been going jelly when he said he was sure they were trying to poison him. He'd gotten rattled, when he kept getting pains in his stomach after eating, and he said they were all watching him, or one would grin and rub his belly. Then Pinto came up on him when he was sleeping, saying only that he heard Pesh yelling in his sleep. Pesh was scared silly when they started pointing forefingers like pistols at him and he ran to Santa Ana, California, where he turned himself into the feds.

Although the law had everything from Pesh, there was nothing they could do. The way the papers put it, the problem was that under state law you can't convict someone for a crime based solely on the testimony of someone else like Pesh who was also involved. It had to be corroborated by an independent evidence or by testimony from someone else. The DA would have loved it if I'd opened up, but I wasn't about to.

Before any of this happened, the DA's guys kept coming around, trying to get me to deal, saying that if I didn't cooperate and testify about what actually happened, I'd get the big max, seven big ones in the slammer. One said, "You seem to be a reasonable guy, an intelligent guy. So why do you want to go to jail?"

I said, "If I have to go to jail, I'll go to jail."

I'd already made court appearances, but Robert Tannenbaum, the Manhattan DA, kept postponing. He was out to get Judge John Murtagh for the trial, knowing that Murtagh would hit me with the max. Blast had done nothing about paying for my lawyers, and that was also bothering me.

After I'd come back on the street, after the three days with my own family, Blast saw me on the block and asked, "How you feeling?"

"All right. Good."

"Cool off a little bit?"

"Yeah," I said. Then I saw the guys, and there was Bobby Darrow among them, watching us.

"Now," said Blast, "I want you to settle this with Bobby in a nice way."

"Listen, Blast. Listen."

"Just do it, for my sake. We need this guy, don't we? Send him on suicide missions, and he goes. If he goes that way and he's taken off, he goes. Fuck him. Am I right?"

"Yeah, Blast, you're right." I thought to myself, what a fucking user.

All the while Darrow was watching us. Blast turned to him. "Bobby, come here."

Darrow wasn't tilted over and he even looked like his old self. I said, "Fuck it. Who needs all this aggravation?" and we shook hands. The guys were all watching. Blast was happy going off, leaving us there. Then as quietly as I could I told Darrow, "Bobby, I'll say hello, I'll say goodbye, but that's as far as it goes. As far as doing anything with you, forget about it."

"What're you—"

"That's it, Bobby. I will never go anyplace with you again."

You could feel that coldness between us. I just walked away from him.

The big kid, Bobby Boriello, came over grinning, taking me by the arm. "See you guys are friends again."

"Yeah, we're friends," I said, and walked away from him too.

Blast was still looking to take off Allie Boy, then arranged to negotiate for a sitdown at the table, only Allie Boy wouldn't be walking away. Allie Boy had done something like fourteen years in the slams, had forgotten too much about the streets, and all I really think he wanted to do was negotiate for peace.

The two Syrians, Louis and Sammy, went to pick him up, had Allie Boy getting in the car, when Jerry Lang grabbed him, yelling, "What the fuck's the matter with you? You go with these guys, you're not coming back."

When the Syrians told us about it at Dolly's, I asked, "Why didn't you just shoot them right there, leave them in the street?"

Louie gave me one of his grins.

"Louie," I said, "you had the pistols on you?"

"Yeah, we had the pistols on us."

"So why in the fuck didn't you shoot the both of them? You had the two of them."

"You know, Greek, lately you're acting funny."

"Yeah. Well, Joey's dead, that's how funny I'm acting," I said.

twenty-three

That summer we were making as if we were watching the Mets on the tube at Roy-Roy's Café, but really we were looking at all the activity across the street with the two Syrians, Sammy and Louie, who kept going back and forth to Blast. Now Punchy was talking to him. You just knew that something was coming off.

At my table Tony Bernardo asked, "What's so fucking important that Blast wants to talk to us about, to stick close?"

"Who the fuck cares?" I said.

We were just sitting there, pretty well disgusted. Roy-Roy wasn't even talking. All sorts of things had happened: pistols were missing from the block, money had been taken from the numbers bank, guys just weren't doing what they were supposed to, and Blast wasn't doing anything about it. The whole thing was damned disgusting.

At Dolly's the numbers sheet, ribbon, and money were always kept in a certain place in the kitchen before being transferred. The ribbon was there but four thousand turned up missing. Any one of the guys involved—Jimmy Springs, Smokey the Bear, Castro, or Tarzan*—could have taken it. The simplest thing would have been to tax them all, but Blast did nothing.

He'd asked the guys, "Did you do your homework, go on surveillance?" And the answer would be they didn't get a chance to, or they weren't feeling good, or they had a date that night with their chick, all sorts of excuses, any one of which Joey would have chased you off the block for, after breaking your head. But then Blast wasn't about to press the crew. He needed them. And being the high bleacher that he was, he wasn't about to move on anything himself.

Then pistols and even personal things were missing, and this was from guys that you would spill blood with, stand up for, go to jail for. Some brotherhood. Blast had to come up with something to hold the crew together, although he was moving right about one thing, and had accomplished it about a week before.

He'd gotten in with two Colombos who started feeding him information. We met with them, making sure not to be made, leery that they were setting us up, or that the information would sucker us into something. But it checked out. It was very good: where guys like Allie Boy, Jerry Lang, and a lot more were making their entrances in and out, where they could be tagged. Despite that, I wasn't all that interested. Too many things had already happened.

It didn't change my feelings one way or the other when Blast came over to us at the table finally and told us something important was going down. Then he said, "Don't want you fellas to feel offended if you're not into it, what's going on, how it's coming off. The less you know, the better. All I'll tell you is we got a guy, a good guy, coming in to do a piece of work."

"Fine," I said, but it didn't change my feelings any.

Afterward two detectives came in, checking us off. One was beefy, something you didn't see much in a cop anymore. In the old days they all looked red and beefy. Now they sort of looked anemic with mustaches and

*Frank DeForte, Mod Squad.

long hair. I guess a lot of things were changing. The
beefy detective asked how the Mets were doing. Tony
Bernardo said, "Lousy. The only thing good about the
game is the commercials."

"Slide, you sonofabitch," he said, and when I
looked I saw the guy tagged at second. Now I was looking across the street at Blast and a couple of the crew.
I kept one good eye on Blast and that huddle. The
other detective was saying something about the stupid
bastard trying to go for a standup double. They both
watched it for a while.

After they'd gone, Punchy came over, grinning.
"Tonight's the night," he said.

"Yeah," I said.

Tony Bernardo said nothing and neither did Roy-
Roy.

"Whatsamatter with you guys?" said Punchy. "You
guys should be happy."

"Yeah, we're happy," I said. "We're always happy."

About an hour went by, and there was Punchy
in the huddle with Blast and Sammy the Syrian. They
were really smiling. Then Punchy came over to us at the
table again. "Why don't you guys turn the radio on?
Go 'head. Turn it on. You'll hear something real interesting."

In the back of Roy-Roy's someone dialed 10-
10, the news station, getting a lot of unimportant stuff.
Then came the news bulletin of a shooting at the Neapolitan Noodle.

"Now listen," said Punchy, smiling.

The announcer went into how four people had
been shot, two killed instantly and two wounded, perhaps critically.

"Hey!" went Punchy, like the Dodgers were still
in Brooklyn and they had just made a grand slam.

The announcer was going into what sort of restaurant the Neapolitan Noodle was, that sort of thing,
when Punchy said, "Come on, give us the names. Jerry
Lang, Allie Boy, Moose, and that fuck Joe Yak."

The announcer started to go into the shooting. I
moved in closer. Roy-Roy was beginning to smile.

The announcer described how the lone assailant, a short, stocky man in his forties, who appeared to be wearing a wig, ordered a drink, then brandished two revolvers, firing nine shots directly at the party of four, killing two and wounding two.

"Hey!" went Punchy. "Now give us the names."

"Killed instantly," reported the announcer, "were Sidney Epstein and Max Tekelch."

"*What!*" went Punchy.

The other two wounded were two other Jewish guys. Whatever was beginning to happen just stopped. It stopped us cold. Tony Bernardo was staring at me, and I must have been staring. Punchy seemed more shocked than any of us, and he asked, "What the fuck *happened?*" Then, "We'd better clean house."

"Yeah," I said, "you'd better do just that."

It wasn't long after that that Bobby Darrow, tilted, came staggering with that hop along the street, his head leaning over to his shoulder. You just knew he had to be in on it, the right guy to eyeball the wrong ones.

Well, we cleaned house, moving the pistols all around, expecting the law to come down on us that night, but they didn't. Afterward I just couldn't sleep thinking over what had happened. I could just see that guy, the out-of-town shooter from Vegas that Blast brought in, holed up at a midtown hotel, and I could imagine Sammy or Louie, and for sure Bobby Darrow, going back and forth, knowing that the Colombos would be coming into the Noodle, and that night they were going to catch them right, tag them good.

The guy just sat there, waiting in his room, waiting for the knock, and maybe Sammy came in saying, "They just went in, all four of them, Persico, Lang, Moose, and Yak, but there's a cop with them," and the guy said, "I don't give a fuck for the cop."

Then Sammy might have said, "It's some relative of Allie Boy's," and maybe the guy said, "That makes it better."

He could have had the one pistol on, got the other one from under the mattress. Maybe that was the last thing he put on after he coated his hands with plastic spray. Maybe he tried his thumb on a water

glass to see if it showed prints, and it came out
smudged without a single line. Then he put on the wig,
and even makeup. Then he was set. Or he had been
set all along, sitting there like a clown with the wig and
makeup, waiting for the knock.

Then there was the possibility that one of the Mod
Squad drove the guy, a kid like Bobby Boriello or
Preston who had the real balls for something like that.
Bobby Darrow waited to eyeball, while the two Syrians
worked the backup. But it couldn't have been them.
They were coming back and forth, all right, but they
were there on President Street when it came off. Some-
body had to be in the backup.

Now here were Allie Boy Persico, Jerry Lang,
Charley Moose, and Joe Yak at the bar, and Allie Boy's
relative, the detective, probably was someplace else
while they talked business. Maybe Bobby D went by
the window and had them eyeballed where and what.
Then he went to the car. The guy was just sitting there,
still like a clown, and Bobby might have said, "Pal, it's
turkey time. You couldn't get them any better," and
told him where and how they were standing at the bar.
Then the guy got out, maybe taking a deep breath and
maybe not. If he was that cool, he didn't do anything.
He would do his work, go back to the hotel, shower,
and eat a steak. Or maybe he'd go right to the airport,
get on his plane, not talking or looking at anyone, and
maybe once it had taken off, he'd go to sleep.

Well, he could do that, all right, and I knew the
sort, a guy who could come at you cold and feel nothing for you, either before or after the work. Just blow
you away, that's all, and at the Noodle he must have
seen the four guys right where they were eyeballed.

What he didn't know was that, probably, the waiter or the maître d' had told the Colombos they had a
table for them now, and when the Colombos moved off
with their party, the four Jewish guys moved up to the
same spot with their wives. That was what the shooter
saw—four guys—exactly as Bobby D had told him.

Maybe the bartender came up to him, planting his
hands in front of the guy, and the guy said, "Scotch
whisky," and maybe the bartender thought there was

something funny about the guy, like he was wearing a wig and seemed embarrassed about it. Or he was too busy to care. Maybe the shooter never touched his drink, but stepped back, pulled two pistols from his waist, and let go.

It jolted the place. It jolted everybody, and everybody ducked, screaming, not even aware of anything, not even seeing the four guys falling, when the shooter just laid the two pistols on the bar, didn't look left or right, just walked out without rushing.

It must have jolted the Colombos. They had to go for cover. That detective, the Persico relative, must have ducked too, and when he came out with the service pistol, there wasn't anybody, just those guys sprawled bloody all over each other and the women screaming. Maybe he tried getting past them, looking for the shooter, shoving by them. There was nothing, not even the door closing or a guy going by the big window. Nothing at all. And when he went out in the street, there was nothing there either, just people running up to the big window to look, and crowds walking along like nothing had happened, just going along.

Well, that's what I thought about all night. That's who we'd taken off—four Jewish guys, four meat dealers. Now two just meat. It was a fucking disaster. The Colombos wouldn't have to do anything. The law would really come at us now.

twenty-four

In the morning it was nice out. You couldn't feel anything. The law was waiting for us outside Roy-Roy's. Homicide detectives came around the car, saying they had to take us down.

I said, "Well, I guess you do."

Over at the precinct on Union, they took four of us at a time into the interrogation room. They had me, Tony Bernardo, Roy-Roy, and Louie the Syrian. The Syrian wasn't smiling as usual. The two detectives said they had to ask the questions, and I said of course. We told them what they expected us to say, that we were all down at Roy-Roy's. One said he couldn't quarrel with that. He'd been watching the baseball game with us, and I told him he was the best eyeball witness that anyone could possibly get. He said nothing. The questions were routine, petty stuff, where we were residing now, that sort of thing. It was something they had to do, that's all, vouching that we had been observed at Roy-Roy's establishment during the incident at the Neapolitan Noodle.

I remembered one of the first times I'd gotten

rousted by the law. It had been during the Profaci war, and I hadn't been made yet as a regular. They probably thought I was an outside guy. Well, Roy-Roy, Little Ang Parfumi, and Cockeyed Dunn had a nymph over at my apartment on Caton Avenue. We were going on her, one at a time, waiting over at Georgie's Restaurant, but the law was waiting to go on us. Seeing my car going back and forth, they thought a hit was coming.

When Little Ang left, they tailed him but lost him. When he got back and I got in, taking the car, I just pulled out when three unmarked cars and a sector car came at me all at once. Pistols drawn, they pulled me out, frisked me, searching the car. Over at the station house they started working me, asking what we were up to, who we were looking to waste. I told them, "Hey, I don't even know what you're talking about. I'm dumb to the whole thing here."

This one detective, a real arrogant, nasty sonofabitch, asked, "You didn't lend your car to Angelo Parfumi?"

"I don't lend my car to nobody."

"You're a fucking liar."

He gave me some whack, knocking me off the chair. Coming off the floor, I wanted to go at him. He said, "I wouldn't advise it."

I took the chair, sitting. "I'm not saying nothing to you guys."

"You don't know Angelo Parfumi?" he said.

"Don't know Angelo Parfumi."

"You don't know anybody from the Gallos?"

"Don't know anybody from the Gallos."

He wanted to go at me again when the desk sergeant said, "His lawyer's on the phone."

"Already?" said the detective, and he looked at me as though he had a different opinion of me.

"Wants to know if we're booking or releasing him," said the desk sergeant.

"We're releasing him. Tell his lawyer"—he was looking at me when he said it—"we're taking him home, checking on his license. I mean, to see if he has one, since he didn't have it with him. We are entitled to do that, aren't we?"

Along with another detective he took me to the apartment. All I needed was for them to come in and find all the heavy hardware, pistols and everything else. In the lobby I told them, "This is as far as you go."

They looked at each other.

"Hey," I said, "I got a broad in there. She's ready. Know what I mean? Listen, with two detectives coming in, it would blow it for me. Would disturb her. Now that wouldn't be right. Why don't you wait here? I'll just get it."

They got in a huddle, and the other detective said, "All right, get it."

"I'll be right back," I said.

Roy-Roy was ready to go out the window. I told him to just stay quiet. The broad was in the bedroom playing with herself. The sheets were a mess, and it looked like the mattress was coming off the bed.

When I came out, the one who'd rapped me was grinning when I handed him the license.

"Okay," he said, looking at it. "I can just imagine what you're thinking."

My mouth was throbbing, already blistered where he'd rapped me. I told him, "Pal, you wouldn't like to know what I'm thinking."

"We'll run into you again," he said.

But that was that. They left. That was the only time I'd gotten a belt from the law.

I know what they do to street guys. It's a lot different when you don't have the connection. You don't just get a belt in the mouth. You get your head, balls, kidneys, and everything else worked over, and you're lucky if your mother can recognize you afterward, and you might not have been nailed for anything heavy.

Get rapped with a pistol and that makes them crazy altogether. Kill a cop? Forget about it. You'd have detectives from every precinct coming over specially to work you, and it would come off that you were resisting arrest when you were already unconscious. And it's not particularly unusual for a cop to kill you, plant a Saturday night special on you, shoot a hole through the side of his jacket, saying that's how close you came to killing him and, of course, the officer had no other recourse but to act, all in the performance of duty.

But a wiseguy, that's different. And it's not simply a question of the law being on the pad, although you do have to shmeer certain guys, a lot of guys, to work right. The two that pulled us in, questioning us on the Neapolitan Noodle, weren't on the schmeer. Maybe the nice treatment was that they were around so much we got to know them well, even about their families and their problems. It was like a special truce, a crazy kind of respect for each other, but no holds barred on everything else. There were few exceptions. The only one I knew of was Steve the Greek.

He was an outside guy, not doing much of anything. In fact, I know he wasn't doing anything other than running errands for Louie the Syrian, just an innocent kid that liked to be around us. One night two off-duty detectives who weren't from the Union Street Precinct—one of them was another relative of Junior Persico—came on the kid. The kid was being pushed around and would have gotten it bad, only we came out of Dolly's yelling, and the usual surveillance teams were on the block. The two had no reason to roust the kid, since he wasn't into anything, but they said they were taking him in.

Well, they took him in, all right, straight to the piers, where they worked him over. I'd never seen anybody beaten so bad. That kid's head was like a swollen balloon with his eyes black and shut, a nose on him like a burned sausage, and a shiny mouth blistered right up to his nose. It wasn't for any reason at all, except that the kid was around us. The only way you could read it was the Colombos sent down Junior's relative and the other bastard to beat the kid, as an example.

Steve the Greek was off the block after that, and I never saw him again. I guess whatever balls the kid had, had been taken right out of him.

Well, after we'd been interrogated, still feeling lousy over the Noodle, I felt like packing and getting the hell away from President Street. I called the wife, asking if she and the kids were okay, but I was even shorter than usual. I didn't say anything about coming home. I knew the phone was still tapped, especially now. That didn't bother me as much as the idea that information was being fed back to the Colombos. It wasn't only the law that could do it, but some guy from the telephone company working for three bills, looking for extras.

The business with the Neapolitan Noodle was all over the papers. Mayor Lindsay was angry, saying that he would chase all the wiseguys out of the city, that he was going to name the vast number of legit businesses tied in with organized crime, and that he was forming a new police division to deal with the problem.

The Noodle had been tied to our crew. Well, about that they were right. I don't imagine Blast would still have the carte blanche from Lindsay that he had when there was that racial problem in Bedford-Stuyvesant. The Italians and the blacks had been going at it, and there had already been a killing. I imagine, since it involved the Italians, Lindsay felt the Gallos could contain it and prevent anymore killings.

I had been by the corner of Columbia and President streets when I saw this Jewish rabbi. I couldn't imagine what in the hell he wanted around there. He said he was looking for the Gallo brothers, and I said, "What Gallo brothers?"

"The Gallo brothers from President Street," he said. "I'm Rabbi Shreiber, and I've been designated by Mayor Lindsay to speak to them."

Maybe the mayor had a sense of humor. Maybe he thought it was something we could understand. It was a rabbi, all right, a real Jewish rabbi, complete with the beard, yarmulka, and all.

"Mayor Lindsay sent you to speak to them?" I asked. "You got any kind of identification?"

He showed it and gave me his card, explaining what it was all about. I told him to go around the corner and park while I spoke to the people he wanted to see.

Larry Gallo and Blast were in the back of Roy-

Roy's, and I told Larry, "There's a rabbi to see you, a Jewish rabbi, a real one. Mayor Lindsay sent him."

"Mayor Lindsay?" said Larry.

"It's about that problem over at Bedford-Stuyvesant," I said, and I explained it all.

Blast was smiling, while Larry, looking at the rabbi's card, said, "Well, it looks innocent enough. Let him come in."

After the rabbi spoke to Larry, Larry designated Blast, who was a good listener at times and a good talker, to see what he could do over there.

When it had been all arranged, we set up a meet with the Italians, to discuss it with a spokesman. Well, when we did go, the law was like an army—white helmets, riot trucks, paddy wagons, and canteen trucks along the way. When we got out of the car, a police inspector stopped us. Blast showed him the letter from Mayor Lindsay, which said, as I remembered it, that Lawrence and Albert Gallo and their associates were not to be stopped, questioned, harassed, or molested by the police at any time, and something about his directive and the aforementioned matter.

Well, the inspector read it, looked up, and said nothing at all, passing it back to Blast. At the restaurant it turned out that Blast had been in the Army with the spokesman for the Italians. There were no threats made as anyone might have supposed. But it did end the troubles right there.

After that, there was another incident in our section of Brooklyn, over by Avenue L. We straightened that out too. Blast was asked to speak on TV, and he made a few statements, and we were being praised by Lindsay, the papers, and suddenly everyone else. With that and the time Larry and Blast saved those Puerto Rican kids from the fire, the Gallos became heroes of sorts, and if the law even so much as started to bother us, people would yell from their windows, "Leave those boys alone! They're good boys!" I guess you could say we received a lot of respect.

But now, after the Neapolitan Noodle, we all had horns, particularly as far as Mayor Lindsay was concerned, and I couldn't say that I blamed him at all.

The following morning, after we'd been questioned about the Noodle, I told Tony Bernardo I was going home, getting the hell out of there. He was washing, and he said, "Think I'll get out of here for a couple days myself. Maybe go to the gummare's, just to get out of here."

He didn't say anything while I packed my bag. He stood watching me, wiping his hands with the towel, then shook his head. "What a fucked-up mess," he said.

"Yeah," I said, taking the bag down off the bed. I didn't feel like doing anything but getting out of there.

He was still watching me. I guess he was one of the few guys in the crew that I still liked and respected.

"Well," I said, "any time you want to get out of this business, you can always pass for Sinatra."

That was another thing about him, the blue eyes, and the dark hair, he did look like Sinatra. Then I remembered Joey nicknaming him Cockhound. I had to think of that too.

I didn't shake hands with Tony B or anything. All I said was, "I'll see you," and he said, "Yeah."

I had the kid, Castro, drive me. But when we got to the intersection, the law was blocking us. There was a bunch of them, all hard-eyed, telling us to get out. The car was given a going over, my suitcase too, and we were patted down. They were part of the special division Lindsay had just set up, and they weren't at all like the usual cops on the block. They were a lot rougher, but not pushing you around or anything. It was just that they hated our guts.

The one who patted me down had me by the arm, watching the others finishing off. Then he said, "Okay, you can go."

"Thank you," I said.

After Castro turned off the block, I looked back to see if we had a tail. Then I wasn't looking at all.

At my apartment I sat out on the terrace, alone. It was a nice day, all right. The Jewish ladies as usual were in their beach chairs in a line, watching everybody. They would have eyeballed those four Colombos better.

My wife and the kids had been glad to see me home. I worried that the kids knew. They didn't know anything. Kitty had seen to that, but she knew, all right. I hadn't gone into anything with her. She could read between the lines. You didn't have to hit her with a hammer. She already knew about the numbers money and pistols disappearing without my telling her. She'd talk to Toni, Blast's wife, or Dottie, Bobby Boriello's, and I guess that's what they'd rap about. Kitty said, "Guys are robbing money? What's happening down there? Now this."

She'd come out on the terrace, closing the door behind her, not saying anything for a long time. She kept looking at me in a very funny way. You could just sense that she wanted to know everything that happened at the Noodle, but she didn't ask anything about it at all.

"What a disaster," I said.

"Yes," she said, and went quiet. Then, "Were you picked up?"

"We were all picked up."

"Figured as much. Well, how does it look now?"

"How could it possibly look?"

She went quiet again.

"Listen," I said, "why don't you take the kids to the beach or something?"

"No. They're playing. They're happy."

"Well, at least they're happy. Can't get worse than this, can it?"

"No, it can't. I'll make you something to eat."

She closed the door behind her. I was alone again. It really was a fine day. It seemed all I had to look forward to was my trial.

twenty-five

The only thing you could say about my trial was that it started in September and it took a month to convict me. Judge Murtagh and DA Tannenbaum had set out to nail me for seven big ones on the gun charge. Murtagh wouldn't even grant us a postponement when Bob Weiswasser's kid was born with a heart murmur and was expected to die. Bob pressed for a postponement, telling the judge that he was too upset to give me the sort of defense he was capable of and I was entitled to. Murtagh granted a postponement only after the baby died. The other thing Murtagh did was allow my parents ten-minute visits and to bring food during recess. Other than that the guy allowed nothing.

Tannenbaum, tall, thin, a sarcastic bastard with glasses who wore his pants so short that they were three inches above his socks, came at me with everything he could, including Salvatore LaMonica, who was the counterman at Umberto's, Sina and her daughter, and Joe Pesh.

LaMonica said that during the shooting he'd gone to the floor behind the counter but afterward saw me with something shiny in my hand. In his preliminary statement he'd said that he'd seen me with a small automatic. No one that I knew talked to the guy.

Sina said she was so terrified that she didn't see anything during the shooting, that she was only trying to protect herself and her child, while her kid, Lisa, as standup as anyone could possibly be, said she hadn't seen me with a gun or anything like that. Tannenbaum remarked that we had even persuaded a child to lie when Lisa pointed her finger at me and said, "But I love him."

Before they brought Joe Pesh into the courtroom, Murtagh warned me not to try to intimidate the witness or to do anything foolish. Bob Weiswasser told me, "I know what you're thinking, and I know how you'll feel when they bring this asshole in. But for God's sake, don't do anything to jeopardize the case. It'll go a lot harder on you. Pete, just don't do it."

"Of course not," I said, but I was shaky waiting for the door to open, to see that sonofabitch.

Here he came with at least six court officers and a dozen federal marshals. There he was in the middle of them, guarded better than Nixon, walking over to the prosecutor's table. I could feel my blood rushing. There he was, the sonofabitch, wearing sunglasses, a lot thinner than that night at Umberto's, and not looking at me at all. But he knew I'd caught every step he'd made. He was already rattled.

The court officers and marshals sealed off the corridors, two marshals behind him, two at the exit by the witness stand, two more standing right behind me. I was really shaking. I wanted to take the eyes out of his head. If I could get my hands on him, I'd crack that big neck of his like a fucking twig. I started to get up when Bob took my arm. "Pete, don't." I shrugged him off. The two marshals got right up behind me. The others were ready to move.

I just walked over to the prosecutor's table. I looked Pesh right in the eye, and I wanted his eyes. But all I did was take the pitcher of water and the cups from the table, all the while looking at him.

Judge Murtagh cautioned me again, saying not to

look at the witness at all. But I looked at him anyway. I put my thumbnail between my teeth and snapped it at the sonofabitch.

Murtagh called my attorneys to the bench, told them that if I did anything else, made gestures of any sort, I would be handcuffed to the chair for the remainder of the trial. Bob kept advising me not to do anything. I was still shaking.

On the stand Pesh told what happened, going into the whole business of eyeballing us and then going over to Pinto at the café. But to *see* him telling it, not just getting it from newspapers or what I'd heard, was something else, when he was the one mainly responsible for Joey's death. I had all to do to keep from killing him right there.

After a recess Pesh didn't want to testify anymore, but he was back on the stand for another two hours. The main thing Tannenbaum was after was that I had a gun.

I took the stand and said that Joey had passed me the gun. Well, Tannenbaum had a medical expert who, in a lot of medical terms, showed that it would have been impossible, that the way Joey had been shot he had lost all mobility.

The jury was finally charged, and instead of the felony, they found me guilty on a misdemeanor, for having an empty weapon. I guess if I hadn't fired it I would have been found guilty of the felony. I heard afterward that they didn't buy Pesh's testimony, but then they didn't buy my story about Joey passing me the piece.

A month later I stood for sentencing. Before getting to me, Murtagh suspended a five-year sentence on a black woman who'd killed her common-law husband with a knife, and suspended five years on a Puerto Rican for a loaded gun. I told Bob he was in a good mood. But I knew I was going away. I'd come in with a packed suitcase. Murtagh gave me what I'd expected, the max on the misdemeanor—one year.

I was remanded to the Tombs, and ten hours later, after being in the worst filth, with roaches and rats, guys screaming, going into withdrawals, I was shipped out to Rikers Island. That was almost as bad as the Tombs.

You could, though, be very comfortable at Rikers. If you made Dorm Seventeen, you were in paradise. They had a regular festa e fame over there, the best of everything: food, booze, pot, and even broads. But that was for guys like Gambino's underboss O'Neil (Dellicroce) and Fat Gigi (the Whale)* from the Harlem crew.

But the rest of Rikers was either maximum security, or stinking dorms, each crowded with over a hundred and sixty guys in double bunks. There was no festa e fame there, just roll-your-owns like Bull Durham, lousy food, and clothes and shoes that looked like they belonged to derelicts. If you had the greens, you could at least get good commissary, but nothing like Dorm Seventeen.

Nicky Gido, an old-timer, was supposed to go there. He was in his sixties, doing a five-month gambling bit, and I think it was the first slam time he ever did other than a usual roust, which was sort of funny. What was funnier, it was my first slam time. Gido had the heavy greens to make seventeen, but just when he was about to be transferred, Rikers had a big shakeup because of seventeen. A hack captain, being investigated, resigned. Gido would have made it, but I never would have with O'Neil, since Joey had once given him a beating at Luna's restaurant. He wasn't about to approve a Gallo in with them, particularly a guy who had been so close to Joey. So Gido and I did our own time like the other guys, blacks and Hispanics—Hispanics who, once you got to know them and got tight with them, would call you compadre, the close one.

Between Rikers, Bedford Hills, and Napanoch, but mostly Rikers, I pulled ten months. Bedford Hills, which had been a women's prison, was minimum security with only a barbed wire fence, a lot better and cleaner than Rikers, and the food was more than decent. But I wasn't there long at all. As soon as they

*Louis Inglese.

found I was OC, organized crime, back I went to Rikers, in the same meat wagon that brought me, freezing with one blanket and nothing much to look out of. My wife, who had come up to see me, saw only the meat wagon pulling away and didn't know until afterward that I'd been on it. Napanoch was better than Rikers. Anything was better. But being city prisoners we were all shipped back when it was turned over to the state. It wouldn't have gone down too well to mix state prisoners doing twenty years and life with city guys doing a couple of months to a year.

At Napanoch one time, when I was in max, I met a Colombo. I hadn't recognized him right off as he'd lost a lot of weight, and he was something like three-hundred-and-fifty pounds when I knew him. He reminded me of the beef I'd settled for him one time. Then asked what tier I was on, what cell, and asked what I needed. I told him I didn't need anything. But he said he'd fix me up with sandwiches every night during water time. At water time the hot water came around for the instant coffee, along with a brown paper bag, the water guy saying it was a present from my friend. It was two tuna fish sandwiches. I had to remind myself that my "friend" was affiliated with Colombo.

I wouldn't touch either of the sandwiches. It looked a lot better than what I was eating. Then I called out to the black guy in the cell next to me. I couldn't see him. "Hey."

"You talking to me, man?"

"Yeah, Jim, I'm talking to you. You hungry?"

"No, man. I just had that big turkey pie, apple pie, all kinds of good pie. Shit, man."

"Got a couple of good sandwiches. Want one?"

"You jiving me? Goddamn right I want one."

"Here it comes," I said, getting it out on the steel platform, pushing it along with the broom. A black hand came out, snapping it right up.

You could hear him taking it out of the bag. He talked with his mouth full. "What's wrong with it?"

"Nothing, man. Just not hungry."

I waited. Then I asked, "How is it?"

"Finger licking, man. Finger licking."

"Yeah?"

I waited fifteen minutes at least. I hadn't heard him hit the floor. I had taken one half from each of the two sandwiches, making one for him. I kept looking at mine. It looked all right. "Hey, Jim."

He was very bright. "Yeah, baby?"

"That was good, wasn't it?"

"Yummy yum tummy, man. Man, you is a decent human person, man."

"Jim, I'm glad you think so," I said.

I waited another ten minutes, and I was hungrier looking at it. Then I said to myself, the hell with it, and I ate it. It was more than all right. I wished I had the other one.

After that I always had sandwiches at water time. I'd still split the sandwiches and wait. One thing, they never turned out to be poisoned. They were anything but poisoned.

Twice I was sent home when my mother had a heart attack, sent back with six hacks, three shotguns with me in the station wagon, and a backup car, met by a patrol car at the hospital, as well as the hospital guards. My mom was in a coma under the plastic oxygen tent. I was back before she ever came out of the coma. I thought I'd never see her alive again. Early the following morning my wife went to the corrections commissioner and got me the second visit. That was my wife, all right, a fighter.

Every visiting day you could count on her to be first, and she'd bring the limit of twenty-five pounds of food, those good browned chickens, the pepperoni, and the sausage. It was like I had my own Dorm Seventeen. But one time she came with very disturbing news.

Whenever she had something important to tell me, knowing that the hacks had the phones tapped in the visitors' booths, she'd write it all out on paper and hold it to the window. This time what she wrote really shook me. The word out on the street was that I had set up Joey to be taken off.

A guy I'd helped out when he was on the lam ran into my wife up in Fishkill and told her that he owed me a special favor, that I should be extra careful when

I hit the streets, that Frankie Blair, the good fellow in the Gambino Family, had sent the word out. Well, I knew why. Frankie Blair had never gotten over it that I'd shot two of his men.

Punchy had a restaurant on Nevins Street, and we'd go in to give a fellow brother some play. One night these two greaseballs from Blair's crew were at a table with a woman. It turned out to be a wife to one. He was complaining to her about his mother-in-law, when the mother-in-law came in, and they started arguing. It wasn't the proper thing to do. Punchy and I went over, and Punchy, in a nice way, said, "Listen, this is a family thing with your wife and your mother-in-law. We'd appreciate it if you take it outside or take it home. Don't do it here in the restaurant."

The greaseball, who was doing all the yelling, was cocky about it, "Hokay, gumba, we take it outside."

When they came back in, and the mother-in-law had gone home, the wife started arguing with the greaseball. Then he started cursing and abusing her. That's when we got up again. This time I talked to the guy. "Hey, take your beef outside or take it home."

He gave me some bullshit guiena talk, got his wife to go home, but when he came over to me, he said real nasty, "Hokay now?"

"No, it's not okay now," I said. "You don't do these things over here."

"Hey, *chi é questo?*"

"Who am I? Come outside and I'll show you who I am."

That's when the two greaseballs got into it, and when I got them out front, I started belting both of them. Just then the Mod Squad pulled up. Stevie Gallo, Bobby and Stevie Boriello, and Preston came out of the car with pipes, busting them, before they even asked what it was all about. Punchy and I had to stop it. One guy was holding on tight to his bloody head, his elbows squeezing down under his chin. The other greaseball had him by the arm. I told them, "Get out of here."

"Get out of here?" said the second. "We be right back."

"Oh, you'll be right back. I'll give you something to come back for," I said, and went right for my car parked in front, grabbing the pistol from my car.

They were already running. "Come here!" I yelled. "Come here!" They were really going, and I took a bead, letting go six shots, clipping one in the leg and the other in the ear.

I didn't know then about the guy with the ear. I knew I'd clipped the other one, when he almost went over and then sort of hopped, grabbing onto his leg before making the corner.

Well, that was a beef, so we had to sit down with Frankie Blair and the two greaseballs. You could see the one who had the bottom of his ear clipped right off, scabbing to a quarter moon. Blair was more or less apologetic about them, saying that they should have conducted themselves properly, that I knew the grease- balls from the other side, that they didn't listen, and he hoped I had no animosity toward them. I said no, not as long as they didn't. Then Blair said it was all for- gotten.

Well, it wasn't forgotten. He'd been waiting for his chance to pay back. Now he was saying it all over the streets that I'd set up Joey.

It was damned disturbing to my wife, and I asked her how anyone could believe a thing like that. She was going to hear a lot of things in the streets, but she knew better than to believe any of it. She knew and I knew that I had nothing to do with Joey's killing. In fact, that's the last thing I would ever want. There wasn't any point in her getting upset. I convinced her of that.

When I went back to my cell, it started to work on me. But it had already started.

I looked at the calendar. It was May. The calendar was dog-eared to August, the months I had to go.

1973

twenty-six

It was a little more than a year after the Neapolitan Noodle when I came home that August. One afternoon I was sitting out on the terrace, just looking around at nothing really while I appraised everything that had happened and everything that had been done. Blast had done nothing for me and my family.

After I'd gone away to do the time, Blast, for Christmas, sent over two hundred bucks for the kids, and a couple of times he sent over fifty dollars for food for the table. He never came up with money for my lawyers or money for my bail bond, not even when Judge Murtagh remanded me during my trail, granting the postponement because my lawyer's kid died, and I was held on an additional five thousand. He never did anything like he was supposed to. It always had to come from my own pocket, or from my friends and relatives, like my mother-in-law, as well as Jimmy and Mary.

Mary was my second cousin, whom I'd grown up with, and Jimmy, her husband, was a beautiful guy, a very successful electrical engineer with a going busi-

ness. When he knew that I had to come up with bread
for my lawyers and keep food on the table and pay all
the bills while I was away, he came up with sixty-five
hundred without any sort of hesitation. And now that I
was out, it wasn't a week when he let me tap him for
another five thousand. That's the kind of family I had.
That's the kind of Family Blast was. Zero. Whatever
money he'd sent I had my wife send back. I had my
own family, not the Family, and that's really what it all
amounted to.

Then my wife, fighter that she was, who really
stood by me all that time, finally spelled it all out for
me one night. You knew it was working on her all
along when she said, "Listen, I know what you've
been through. I know what you'll be confronted with.
I know what I've been through, what the kids have
been through. But I'm going to tell you in very simple
terms that if you decide to go back with the Gallos, I
will divorce you."

"Come on, Kitty. You don't mean that."

"Let me say it. I'm finally getting the nerve to say
it. But as much as I love you, as much as you love me
and love the kids, I'll leave you. This is no life for you
or the kids. You're being used, they used you, and Albert will always use you and everybody else. That's
what I wanted to say, what I always wanted to say."

I didn't say anything for a long while. Then I
said, "You really mean it."

"Yes, I mean it."

"You're really something, all right," I said. "Now
you want to listen to me? Do you have faith and trust
in me?"

"I do, you know I do."

"All right. Now I'm going to tell you. I don't owe
any allegiance to anybody down there. I owed it only to
Larry, then to Joey. They were the boss. But they're
dead, and I owe nothing to the Gallos. Blast is not a
boss, and he didn't do the right thing. He didn't take
care of you and the kids, like he was supposed to, or
put food on the table, pay the rent, or even send a
package. So he's a nothing as far as I'm concerned.
But this, I have to do it my way, nicely, quietly, then

I'll pull away. As long as they haven't sent for me, I'm just going to wait."

Three weeks after I was home they did send for me. Roy-Roy Musico and Stevie Gallo came over to the house. I saw them getting out of the car, and I got behind my door before they rang. Roy-Roy was trying to see me from behind the door. "Hey!" he went, grabbing me.

They both gave with the brotherhood hugs and kisses. There was Stevie Gallo, the baby face, that mod dapper look, with his father Larry's big diamond ring, and the usual dirty shoes. Roy-Roy had let his thick hair grow really long and had a full turned-down mustache. Roy-Roy was saying, "Jesus, Greek, you look terrific."

"I feel terrific."

He ran his hand over my beard. "When did you grow that?"

"Rikers," I said.

"Looks terrific. Stevie, don't it look terrific?"

"Yeah, real good. Nobody'll make you with that."

"Sit down," I said. "What can I offer you? Beer, scotch?"

"Yeah, we'll have something," said Roy-Roy.

After I set up drinks along with a six-pack on the coffee table, Roy-Roy asked, "How come you didn't come down?"

"Roy-Roy, don't ask me that. Don't ask me why I didn't come down. What's your purpose in coming here? Tell me. Does Blast want to see me? You know my differences with him."

"Yeah."

"Well, I'd rather not discuss them with you. If he wants to see me, I'll come down and see him."

"Yeah. Well, you know. You want to come down now?"

"No. I'll be down tomorrow."

"Hey, whatever you want. When you're ready to come down, you come down. If you want us to take you now, we can drive you."

"No, I'll cab it," I said.

There was a lot of how's everything, how's everybody feeling, and I said fine, and they said good, and I looked good, and more brotherhood hugs and kisses before they left. But I felt nothing for them, particularly for Stevie Gallo.

When I had been at Rikers, I heard how he and Stevie Boriello came on the owner of a club in Brooklyn, a friend of mine, after having a fight in the place the night before, telling him that if he had any money to send to me, they'd send it. All they were looking to do was shake him down, looking for what other enterprises of mine they could take over. That more than disappointed me about Stevie Gallo. I'd always liked the kid. It turned out that he was no different than the rest of them.

The following day I had the cab let me off a block away from President Street. Everything looked much smaller, even more crowded, and dirtier than I'd remembered. I saw a grubby boarded-up tenement with graffiti all over it, and something in Spanish. It was hot and people were out. Then I saw some of the guys. They weren't making me at all with the beard. The first one who did was Louie the Syrian. I saw him staring, nudging Cousin Tony.

"Hey, Greek," said the Syrian. "That you?"

"That's me."

They both hugged and kissed me. Other guys came over between there and Dolly's, guys like Tony Bernardo, Mooney, and Gerard. I was surprised to see Gerard down there. A Gallo, he had gone over to the Colombos. Now he was back a Gallo. Who was Blast going to bring back in next? Nicky Bianco?

Inside Dolly's Blast came in giving me the brotherhood hugs and kisses, slapping me on the back, saying how terrific I looked, all that bullshit, talking about things like beefs he'd heard I had in the can, then saying the beard looked real good on me. Then he asked, "How long you going to keep it?"

"As long as I feel like it," I said.

After Papa Gallo came and greeted me as well, Blast said, "Pete, let's go to my place and rap a little bit."

Over at Blast's apartment we were alone, not saying much of anything, until he asked, "What I'd like to know is what your outlook is, what you intend to do."

"Don't understand what you mean about my intentions. But I'm going to be very honest with you like I've always been, Blast. First of all, my family wasn't taken care of the right way."

"What do you mean?"

"Exactly that."

"You mean, your wife—"

"Listen, Blast, listen."

"Tony Bernardo was designated to bring fifty dollars a week, every week, for table money."

Yeah, I thought, and fifty a week is about half of what you get if you're on unemployment. But I said, "My wife never saw fifty dollars a week, just a couple of times, and she sent it back."

"I don't understand."

"Blast, I don't want to go into that."

"Okay, let's not go into that."

"All I care about now is I'm out, I'm home, and my only concern is my family. As far as doing any work, I have no intentions of doing anything, unless *I'm* going and *my* family is going to benefit all the way. But if I do anything, I'm going to do it with you and Tony Bernardo, and nobody else in this crew but you and him."

"All right."

"You made a vow and I made a vow that you and I would kill Sonny Pinto. So whenever he's found, I'll be more than happy to go and do it with you."

"I can understand that."

"As far as anything else, don't call me."

"Well, I just wanted to know where you're at. There's a few things in the fire."

"I'm not interested right now. I'm too pissed off."

"What else are you pissed about? Whatever you got to say, say it now."

"Blast, you're out to pick my head. Don't pick my head. What's on your mind?"

"Well, nothing really."

"Nothing really? Isn't something bothering you? Weren't you bothered when I went close with Joey? Weren't you just a little more than perturbed about that?"

"No. What's the difference if you were with him or with me? We were brothers, weren't we?"

"Yeah, but that's not the way it was when we were down here and things were going in the street. You weren't too happy that I was with Joey. Are you blaming Joey's death on me?"

"No. I would never think anything like that."

"Then why is it, Blast, that you and I can't see eye to eye? Because I'm not a gofer? I only go for myself and my family. Whatever I do, I'll do for them.

"You brought in that John, that fucking chickenshit consigliere, the most weaseling, scurmiest motherfucker that ever walked President Street. A guy like that we had to make appointments with to see you? What kind of bullshit was this when we ate shit and dirt together, bled together, and you put a guy like this in front of all the guys down here? Why shouldn't I be pissed off? I've got every reason in the world to be pissed."

"Ah, come on. That's all over with, water under the bridge."

"Well, I just wanted you to know where I'm at."

"All right, good." He went into his pocket, coming out with a roll, counting off five hundred dollars, holding it out to me.

"No, Blast. I'm not taking that money. I don't want any money from you."

"Come on. That's an insult if you don't take it. Don't be like your wife."

"My wife's got a good head on her, and I don't go against her when she's right, when she stood by me a hundred percent and she was more standup than people are supposed to be in the Family. So I could never go against her when she's right. But I'm the one who told her to return the money to you."

"Yeah, all right. But take this money. Come on. Put it in your pocket, buy some clothes, or get the kids something."

"No, Blast."

"If you don't take this, you're going to hurt me, you'll insult me very much."

"Well, if you feel that way about it, give it to me."

I took the five hundred.

Afterward, at Dolly's, the crew came up with the bullshit of a cake with a candle, the cake in red reading "Welcome Home Pete." I had all to do to keep from getting hysterical laughing. Then, when I looked at the phone booth, I remembered the time Joey shot it up, when he shook Bobby Boriello for coming up with excuses.

When I was about to leave, Blast said, "Don't make yourself a stranger down here. Do me a favor. Come down two or three times a week, whenever you feel you want to come down."

"All right, I will."

"So when can I expect you?"

"I'll be down in a couple of days."

"Okay, good," he said.

I wondered how I could hate this guy so much when it had been the opposite with Joey. Well, Blast was the opposite.

A lot of things were hitting me, not only seeing President Street again but feeling it was like a foreign place all of a sudden. The street had changed and I guess I'd changed too.

I found myself walking around some of the old streets. Passing an empty schoolyard with all the graffiti on the walls, I could picture Joey as the blond-haired twelve-year-old runt. I could even hear him the way he sounded then.

I decided to get the hell away from there and hailed a cab, only it got hung up in traffic, and we were just standing when a pack of Puerto Rican kids came zigzagging, making faces at the people in the cars. One kid, a small runt, as cocky as Joey had been, beat on the hood of the cab with his fists. The cabbie yelled at him saying afterward that those goddamned kids were headed for trouble, and I said, "Yeah, maybe they are. What else is there?"

twenty-seven

Two days later I was down at Dolly's, talking to some of the crew whom I hadn't seen the first time, when Little Ang Parfumi said, "Wasn't that a fucking shame what happened to Darrow?"

"No," I said, "it wasn't a shame. It figured that way all along."

It had happened in March, while I'd been away. Bobby Darrow had killed a guy in a ginmill called the Broadway Pub. It wasn't over anything at all, wasn't business, a useless killing. Darrow was probably high on something, and the guy named Sam, who was managing the place, must have given him mouth, that's all. Darrow was hit with the big one, life, doing his time in Attica. Well, that would have happened sooner or later, or somebody would have killed him. Either way he was dead.

We were talking about it when Blast came in, and I told him, "Listen, there's something bothering me which I didn't get into the first time we talked."

"Yeah, what is it, Pete?"

"Let's go over to your place and talk," I said.

At his apartment I told him, "You know there's word, which doesn't sit too good with me, which Frankie Blair is giving out, that I set up Joey at Umberto's."

"Come on, Pete. Where the fuck did you hear this?"

"Blast, this guy is sending out the word on the street. It's not coming from me. I want to talk to this guy."

"Listen, you don't think for one minute that anyone believes that, do you? You know and I know you had nothing to do with it. Not only did we do our own investigation—"

"Wait a minute. What do you mean by that?"

"Well, you know, we had to investigate certain things."

I took a good long look at him. "Are you saying you also investigated *me?*"

"Well, not directly. You were part of it. We had to find out what happened."

"Yeah, but what are you telling me, that you had to find out?"

"You know we always do our own investigations."

"I know that."

"And of course we had to—not investigate, but find out certain things. We knew this was no setup or anything like that."

"But Frankie Blair is opening his mouth. Why? He's got to have a reason. Because I shot two of his guys? Is that why? Well, I got to talk to him."

"He's going to deny it to your face anyway."

"I know he's going to deny it. But I just want him to know that *I* know."

"You're only wasting your time. He's not important."

"He's important to me, Blast. I got to let him know that I know that he's saying certain things. Because he's a good fellow, he's going to deny it? Don't mean a fucking thing to me. But I want him to know. I want to bring my point across to him, Blast."

"It's a waste of time."

"Okay, if that's the way you feel about it, let's forget about it."

"It's not that important."

"I know, there are a lot more important things to be done. In the meantime nothing's getting done."

"Not exactly. We're going to do a piece of work. Want to come in on it?"

"What?"

"We got an appointment with Allie Boy. But we can't leave him in the street. We got to bury him."

I looked at him. Allie Boy again? Again Allie Boy? This guy's got me talking to myself. Joey gets killed, I get shot, and nothing happens, except that fuckup at the Noodle. From then till November, when I go away to do time, nothing happens. Ten months I'm in the can, nothing happens. I'm out and everything wants to happen with me. Instead of saying any of that, I asked, "What's up?"

"Remember the time you dug a hole upstate with Darrow for the guy we were going to lay away?"

"Yeah."

"Reopen it. Want it set for Allie Boy. Take Tony Bernardo with you."

I was still talking to myself. Then he said there were peace negotiations going on, that it was being set up with the Commission for the sitdown. That didn't go together. We're taking off Allie Boy, and at the same time he's talking peace negotiations with the Colombos, except by burying Allie Boy and not leaving him in the streets, the negotiations would go on. But was that hole for Allie Boy or for me?

Early the next morning, while I waited for Tony Bernardo, it didn't sit too well with my wife to see me in a workshirt and jeans. She was in the kitchen, just stirring her coffee, and had been for a long time. You could see she was very far away. I told her, "Kitty, nothing's happening."

She didn't say anything. "Pete," she said finally, "I love you, but I told you, if you're going back, when

you come home one day, you're not going to find me
and the kids."

I didn't say anything for a long time. Then I said,
"I know what I'm doing."

"Well, I don't."

"Listen to me a minute. I can't just pull away.
You know that. I've got to do it my way, pull away
gradually. I told you that. I'll find the shot and I'll
leave, and you'll be right behind me. Trust me, believe
in me."

She took both my hands and held on.

I said, "Well, I'd better see if he's here yet."

It was just about eight o'clock when Tony Bernardo pulled up front. I'd made sure I'd taken a pistol,
a small caliber, strapping it to my ankle. I wasn't
trusting anyone now.

Tony Bernardo was checking out the street, looking around in his seat, when I slid in alongside him. He
took money from his pocket. When he drove me home
the night before, he'd promised to have the twenty-five
hundred. That was money long coming to me from a
union deal.

"Listen," he said, "can I give you twenty-two instead of the twenty-five now? I'll come up with the rest,
but I need the three hundred now."

"Yeah, okay." I stuck the money in my pocket.
"Wait here a minute."

Back in my apartment I told Kitty, "Here's what
you were supposed to get almost a year ago."

"You had to come out of jail before he gave you
this money," she said. "What did he say? Did he even
bother explaining it?"

"Well, he didn't want a woman to know any of
his business," I said.

I'd worked a couple of union deals with Tony
Bernardo. One had been an optical outfit, a big operation in Queens that was having a problem with the
union. I was put onto, to talk to the two partners and
the union delegate. The delegate, a short, stocky guy,
well spoken, had the pickets out and the outfit was shut
down. Tony Bernardo and I took him aside and I told

him, "Believe we have some mutual friends who are associated."

"Possibly," said the delegate.

"Well, before we get into any sort of negotiations, I'd appreciate it very much if you took off the picket line—call who you have to call for an appointment, so we can speak to them."

"Well, I'd like to call."

Tony Bernardo nodded, and I told the delegate, "By all means. That would be just fine."

The call was made. The pickets were taken right off. The two partners never expected anything so fast. I told them, "Well, we do have an appointment with somebody who can resolve this whole matter for you, and of course we'd like to assist you in every possible way we can. But before we talk price, what are you looking for?"

The partners were looking to pull away from the union completely. We could do it for them, but it would take a whole year. Let them sign up for their year contract now, and a couple of months before the contract terminated we would negotiate to get them into another union, get them a sweetheart contract. They were happy about that, all right, one partner saying he wasn't so amazed when one considered the influence we could assert.

Every union works with the mob, since a lot of them, like the teamsters, are mob-connected anyway. All—and I mean all—big businesses that ever have a union problem look to connect up, to get that sweetheart contract, to hire and fire who they want, throw all their people off the welfare and pensions rolls and put themselves and their relatives on it, anybody they wanted, and pay new people just the minimum wage.

The only businesses that never have union problems are those owned by the mob. When the unions try to come in, find out who is affiliated, they back right off. A delegate will be told, "Listen, cousin, we're in the same field." The delegate says they need a contract. "Sure," says the wiseguy, "you'll have a contract, a sweetheart contract."

Well, for that optical outfit, we kept the appointment, going over to a union hall in Brooklyn to talk to his big union guy. Since this was after Joey was killed, we didn't know what we'd be walking into, or who we'd be coming up against. The guy had someone with him in his office who was three times as big as me. Tony Bernardo did the talking since he'd dealt with them before. Although the union guy had nothing to do with it, since it was a sister union striking the optical outfit, he did tell the delegate to cooperate with us, and when I said there were greens here, he said he wasn't looking for any money. He was only too glad to help. That was all it took to straighten out that outfit.

Another union deal involved a sweater manufacturer in the garment district in Manhattan. The partners of the optical house had put us onto it. This guy named Bernie was looking to get away from a union, which he claimed was Communist. He couldn't fire, he couldn't hire, he wasn't his own man. The deal we offered him was that it could all be done legally.

First his company would go into bankruptcy, lose its corporation name, and open a new factory in Jersey, where we'd set him up with another union. He wanted to know a figure. We gave a figure of thirty thou to set it up, ten in front, ten in negotiations, and the other ten when it was settled.

We got in touch with another union guy we knew who was respected and liked in the garment industry. He said we were throwing him a tough one, but he knew there was bread to be made here and arranged to have Bernie come down to the union hall, a small AFL-CIO affiliate. When Bernie met with everyone, including the delegate and the attorney, he knew we weren't just fingerfucking him, and the next day he came up with five thousand, promising to come up with the other five by the end of the week.

At that time my case was already gone and I was up for sentencing in two days, so I told Tony Bernardo to make sure my wife got the money. In all the time I was away, he'd never sent anything to her. I was dealing with a degenerate gambler, the worst degenerate gambler there is, and I knew he'd blow it at the track, and once when my wife visited me at Rikers I told her to tell him I wanted to see him. When Tony B came to Rikers, I asked, "What the fuck's happening, Tony?"

"Well, Jesus, the thing's not set right now. Hasn't gone through. Hey, when I get the greens out, I'll give 'em to your wife."

Well, he didn't, and I knew Bernie had come up with the other five thousand a week after I saw him the last time, and he was still due to pay us another ten. Even when I came home and he knew I was home, Tony Bernardo didn't come up with the money or even call me about it until I came down to President Street. That was just another thing that got me disgusted.

That morning, driving up to Fishkill, we stopped at a garden supply, picked up shovels, a pick, and a bag of lime. When we came up to the spot where Darrow and I had dug the first hole, Tony Bernardo was looking all around. A cornfield was to our left, the corn very high, and we were right by a country road. Beyond that, a good hundred and fifty feet, was the highway.

Spitting on my hands, rubbing them together, I grabbed the pick. All the while I was watching Tony B.

"This where you dug the other one?" he asked.

"Yeah. Want to see where? I'll show you."

"No. I don't like it. Anybody buried here?"

"If they are, you can't see them."

"Don't like it. Road's right here. Anybody passes, they can see us."

"They'll think we're farmers."

"Yeah, we look like farmers, making a hole that looks like just what it is. I don't like this spot."

I stopped with the pick. "Well, if you don't like it, we won't dig it."

"I just don't like it at all," he said.

I was watching him. He just didn't like the spot, that's all. If I had really felt Tony B was setting me up, I would have left him in the hole. It was a hell of a thing when you had to think like that, especially about a guy you'd been close with. There really wasn't much left when you had to think like that. All we did was keep on digging, not saying much of anything after that.

twenty-eight

I started making arrangements to pull out. I was to leave first, then have my family follow. But I had to get some greens together, and I had to make sure I could get a passport and had a fugazy story in case anybody found I was going for a passport.

The fugazy, the bullshit story, was that I was out to work rich Greeks, and the only rich Greeks are in Greece. With all the shipping magnates there, there was a lot of bread to be earned. Well, I talked to Tony Bernardo about it, and I talked to Blast. When they heard money—go!

As soon as my passport came through, I made arrangements to fly to Athens with Little Georgie from Greek Town. I had my airline ticket and was ready to board when I called President Street for the last time. Roy-Roy answered.

"Hi, Roy?" I said.

"Yeah yeah. Who's this?"

"The Greek."

"What's up?"

"Something came up. Very important. Have to

take off. Just tell Tony B I'm on my way. He knows where."

"Okay."

I hung up. It was all over, just like that, finished. Little Georgie stood off while I kissed my wife before boarding, and that was it.

Well, it was all over and done with. During the following year I read and heard what had happened to the Gallos. Negotiations had broken down just about the time I'd left, and it was open warfare.

Stevie Cirillo was killed at a crap table in a Brooklyn synagogue during their Las Vegas night. Sammy the Syrian and Gerard were shot outside the club on Fort Hamilton Parkway, while Mooney, who was with them, wasn't hit at all. Gerard got it in the knee, shoulder, and cheek, while Sammy got it in the calf. Then Louie the Syrian was shot in the head, but he lived. Then Punchy, while he was talking to Jimmy Springs, was shot in the neck, not far from where Louie the Syrian had been shot.

The way they were set up, the Colombos had to have information. I knew Gerard went on the lam afterward, and people thought he was back with the Colombos, that he had been the one leaking the info. But a guy doesn't take three bullets, one right in the face, if he is.

I asked myself what was happening. All the guys were good window men. They weren't so stupid to let you tag them. They'd spot you in a store window, or a rear-view mirror. Somebody had to be tipping off the Colombos about when they would be at certain places.

One hit didn't make sense. Both Gerard and Sammy had been clipped, all right, but not Mooney, who was the made man. He was the logical target. I began wondering about that, all right.

Mooney had been Larry Gallo's partner, and by rights, since he was the only made man down there, the Family belonged to him. Then I thought back to that time at the San-Su-San when Mooney told Darrow and myself to come in with him. "Listen," he had said, "anything you want with me, you'll get it. Ask Blast, and you ain't going to get it. If you go to jail, Blast ain't going to take care of you. But come in with me, you'll get anything you want."

Now I was putting some things together. There was always animosity between him and Blast. After the peace talks broke down, all of a sudden guys were getting clipped one after another. Who had inside information? Who knew their patterns, where they'd be at certain times? Mooney. Who was looking to grab the Family? Mooney. There wasn't much left to grab down there, and anybody who was that crazy to grab on without knowing how to hold it would be in a lot of trouble. That crew, you can live with them for the next fifteen years and you can't trust them.

But what's left? Ricky DiMatteo was in jail. Sammy the Syrian went to Buffalo and he'd been Blast's right hand after Joey was killed. When he wound up back in Brooklyn, he was with Mooney. Louie the Syrian comes and goes. Punchy is an independent. He'll go with whoever is the winner, whoever has the greens. Tony Bernardo can't go with Mooney, since he can't get along with him, so he has no choice but to stick with Blast. Who else is left down there? Not much, just the Mod Squad mostly.

Colombos were found shotgunned, and one was found in an oil drum floating in the river. But not one of them was a Gallo hit. It was just old beefs being settled up by their own crews or others, a good time to throw it on the Gallos. So when you tallied it up, and you counted Joey's killing and my getting shot, the score was them seven and us zero, and I was the only one who went to jail out of Joey's hit.

Joe Brancato, an ex-marine, the toughest mother in the Colombo Family, who had been tied in with Sonny Franzese's crew out in Suffolk on Long Island, had gotten the Colombo crown. He stayed low while people like Vinnie Aloi and Charley Moose scrambled for the throne. He was slick, all right. He was keeping himself well out of it. Our crew never even considered whacking him out. But now Brancato has the throne, and he's going to hold onto it.

Peace negotiations are going on right now, and

since the offer is that Blast and a couple of others will be made, Blast will go for it. They'll all settle up, and then, quietly, Blast will be taken off, as well as the nephew, Stevie Gallo. They won't leave the Gallo name on the streets, that can always be a threat to them one way or another. And that will be the end of the Gallo Family, the final end.

I don't know if it was Little Georgie from Greek Town who got me on the idea of going to Athens, or if he put it in my head to get some writer to tell it the way it really was. Maybe it was all that ridiculous nonsense of Marta Orbach and Joey's memoirs that got me onto it, or maybe it was just reading all the crap I have read about Joey.

Looking back on it now, even the nothing Joey would have given Marta would have been a lot better than most of the things that were ever written about him. I don't think there ever was a don, even Luciano, that people wrote more books about, made movies about, or wrote up in the newspapers than Joey Gallo. Practically everything reads like it had been worked over by some cuckoo clock of a broad on coke, off by ten miles.

Joey was supposed to have been crazy, and he did crazy things, but it really was that he had the balls of a big elephant, standing up to anyone, and that was really why wiseguys hated him, because when he came on street he was exactly what they were all supposed to be.

I'd never seen one to measure up to him, not even Chin, and he was one bad dude, one of the few I respected. Blast never measured up to a third of Joey, and Blast did turn out to be a user, all for himself, and he was no better than Colombo and Profaci, the very thing Joey hated.

Larry Gallo was something else altogether. Now there was a beautiful guy, and I liked him very much, a guy you respected, and when he told you to do something, you did it, and you never once came up with kid excuses as they did with Blast.

So I guess there was a lot you could say about

things like that. Or how wiseguys live off their reputations. Just say "Mafia" and on comes the trembler, the cagetta. But they don't tell you how they scrounge for nickels and dimes, or how they hustle some drunk for fifteen bucks for a cup of coffee, or sell fireworks to kids, or how they blow the rent money on their gummares even before putting food on the table for their kids. They'd rather you thought they all dealt with honor and respect, all that crap, and that they all were right out of *The Godfather*. Well, unless you really are the big don, there's not much to look forward to in this business except being very dead.

It was finished, and I guess really it was finished a long time ago. A lot of times I think about Joey, especially now. I loved that fucking guy.

I still see him in my head—the fight outside the schoolyard, or the business of punching the horse, and, what made it all a circus almost, the lion and Armando the Dwarf. And then seeing him coming out of Sing Sing, which started the whole thing with Colombo. Then remembering what Joey always used to say to me when we'd leave him off by his door. This time, though, I said to to him. "Stay loose, be cool, and I'll see you tomorrow."

ABOUT THE AUTHORS

PETER DIAPOULOS was a member of the Gallo family for many years.

STEVEN LINAKIS shares a Greek heritage with his co-author of *The Sixth Family*. Highly acclaimed as a novelist, he is best known for his brilliant novel of World War II, *In the Spring the War Ended*. His second novel, *The Killing Ground*, was published in 1970. He now lives in upstate New York.

RELAX!
SIT DOWN
and Catch Up On Your Reading!

☐	BLACK SUNDAY by Thomas Harris	(2100—$1.95)
☐	THE MONEYCHANGERS by Arthur Hailey	(2300—$1.95)
☐	ASPEN by Burt Hirschfeld	(2491—$1.95)
☐	THE EAGLE HAS LANDED by Jack Higgins	(2500—$1.95)
☐	RAGTIME by E. L. Doctorow	(2600—$2.25)
☐	THE ODESSA FILE by Frederick Forsyth	(2964—$1.95)
☐	THE BELL JAR by Sylvia Plath	(6400—$1.75)
☐	DRAGONARD by Rupert Gilchrist	(6452—$1.75)
☐	FAMILY SECRETS by Rona Jaffe	(6464—$1.95)
☐	THE DAY OF THE JACKAL by Frederick Forsyth	(7377—$1.75)
☐	ONCE IS NOT ENOUGH by Jacqueline Susann	(8000—$1.95)
☐	THE MANNINGS by Fred Mustard Stewart	(8400—$1.95)
☐	JAWS by Peter Benchley	(8500—$1.95)
☐	TINKER, TAILOR, SOLDIER, SPY by John Le Carre	(8844—$1.95)
☐	THE DOGS OF WAR by Frederick Forsyth	(8884—$1.95)
☐	THE HARRAD EXPERIMENT by Robert Rimmer	(10357—$1.95)
☐	THE LOVE MACHINE by Jacqueline Susann	(10530—$1.95)
☐	BURR by Gore Vidal	(10600—$2.25)

Buy them at your local bookstore or use this handy coupon for ordering: